WORDS WITH RHYTHM

By the same author

THE DESERT IS MY OASIS

WORDS WITH RHYTHM

Second Beat

HISHAM ALI HAFIZ

Translated into English by
Farouk Luqman

Foreword by Bruce Ingham

KEGAN PAUL INTERNATIONAL
London and New York

First published in 1995 by
Kegan Paul International Ltd
UK: PO Box 256, London WC1B 3SW, England
Tel: (0171) 580 5511   Fax: (0171) 436 0899
E-mail: books@keganpau.demon.co.uk
Internet: http://www.demon.co.uk/keganpaul/
USA: 562 West 113th Street, New York, NY 10025, USA
Tel: (212) 666 1000   Fax: (212) 316 31900

Distributed by
John Wiley & Sons Ltd
Southern Cross Trading Estate
1 Oldlands Way, Bognor Regis
West Sussex, PO22 9SA, England

Columbia University Press
562 West 113th Street
New York, NY 10025, USA
Tel; (212) 666 1000   Fax: (212) 316 3100

© Hisham Ali Hafiz 1995

Phototypeset in 10 on 12pt Palatino
by Intype London Ltd

Printed in Great Britain
by TJ Press, Padstow, Cornwall

All rights reserved. No part of this book may be reprinted
or reproduced or utilized in any form or by any electronic,
mechanical or other means, now known or hereafter invented,
including photocopying and recording, or in any information
storage or retrieval system, without permission in writing
from the publishers.

ISBN 0–7103–0547–8

British Library Cataloging in Publication Data
Hafiz, Hisham Ali
  Words with Rhythm: Second Beat
  I. Title
  821

ISBN 0–7103–0547–8

Library of Congress Cataloging–in–Publication Data
Hafiz, Hisham Ali, 1931—
    [Kalimāt lahā īqā . English]
    Words with rhythm : second beat / Hisham Ali Hafiz.
      194pp. 21cm.
      ISBN 0–7103–0547–8
      I. Title.
    PJ7828.F49K3513   1996
    892'.716—dc20   95–29994
                                                    CIP

CONTENTS

Dedication	ix
Special Dedication	xi
Preface	xiii
Foreword by Bruce Ingham	xv
PART ONE To You God, My Praise and Gratitude	**1**
Praise and Gratitude to You	3
Praise Be to God	4
Only God Is Perfect	6
My Memory and Question Marks	7
It Is by the Remembrance of God	11
PART TWO I Love You, I Love You, I Love You! Beloved Messenger of God	**15**
Story of the Marriage of the Virtuous Lady and the Trustworthy Man	17
How Much Do I Love You, Darling	36
I Love You, First, Second, and Third	38
PART THREE People, Listen and Comprehend	**49**
A Lentil Soup River	51
No Way out Without Blood	54
The Fire Under the Ashes Burn All!	56
It Bit My Hand!	58
The Forbidden Food Banquet	60
PART FOUR Philosophical Thoughts and Meditation	**63**
That Unknown	65
True Love?!	67
Negative and Positive	69
Music	71
The Cat and I!	73
The Virgin?!	75

He Made Me Lose Faith in Dreams!	78
When He Knocked at My Door …	80
We're Getting Close to the End!	82
A Paradise Made of Plastic	83
In Reality and on Paper	85
How Can Summer and Winter Meet?	88
The Reign of Frivolity	90
The Noose	92
PART FIVE Bewildered Sighs	95
Would I Find a Medicine?	97
I Find Shelter in Silence	100
This Is My Tragedy	103
Days	105
I Want to Die Standing	107
Prisoner of a Mirage?!	108
Especially You, Enemies	109
Desperate Hope	110
I Have Decided Not to Sleep	112
It Was My Heart That Cried	113
I Don't Know, I Cannot Tell	115
PART SIX I? Who Am I?	117
I? Who Am I?	119
Am I a Beast or a Human Being	121
I Am a Different Beast!	124
No Doubt I Am the Madman!	125
We, the Artist, Sanctify Freedom	128
You, I, and Time!	130
PART SEVEN You and I Are Adam and Eve!	135
You and Me	137
You and My Imagination	139
Adam and Eve 1	141
Adam and Eve 2	143
Adam and Eve 3	144
Adam and Eve 5	145
Adam and Eve 7	147
Adam and Eve 9	149

Adam and Eve 11	151
Adam and Eve 13	153
Adam and Eve 14	154
Adam and Eve 17	156
Adam and Eve 18	158
She: No and Yes	160
With You, I Drown	163
Fed Up With Questions, You Fake the Answers	165
If You Leave Me	167
I Love You	170
I Look Down, I Behave Arrogantly	172
This is My Tragedy	174
PART EIGHT Characters and Images	177
Tyrants	179
A Tyrant and a Mufti	182
Banquet of the Mean	184
I Don't Know Why	185
The Labour of Sedition	187
The Secret	190
Index of First Lines	193

Dedication

The way you received
Words with Rhythm
Gave me a joy.
Your comments
Took me by surprise.
Your phone calls,
Letters,
And words,
And all that I heard about it
From you
Were soothing and comforting.
It was all this that stimulated me,
Stirred up my emotions,
Kindled my fires,
And made me
Try again,
Collecting something
Of the past, of the present,
And of the future
To launch a new satellite
Far into space,
So you may receive its signals,
Which are tender or furious,
Regretful or content;
Often melancholic,
Rarely happy;
All trying to find a guide
Who would point out
The road to salvation.
?!
?!
I thank you
Again and again,
And again I thank you,
My readers.

Special Dedication

My beloved,
My inspirer,
Most beautiful woman on earth,
You are more tender
Than tenderness itself,
Kinder than kindness,
And warmer than warmth.
You have captivated my mind,
With my full consent
And satisfaction.
You have claimed ownership
Of my heart,
With the first sip,
The first glance.

I am your servant,
Your slave,
And your captive.
You order, and I obey.
You ask, and I comply.
You take me wherever you wish;
You only have to gesture
With your finger.

I am your words,
Your expressions,
Your poetry.
I am your wishes,
Your desires.
And I am in your hands,
And at your feet.
I love you, I love you, I love you,
Mother!

Preface

Day after day, I read
What you jot down
And feel confused
And puzzled;
One day you are
An old man with grey hair,
Rejecting reality,
And on some other day,
You are a young man
Full of piety and repentance.
Everyday you are
Someone different.
You change your tone:
Today you are a boy
On the offensive
Or an adolescent,
And tomorrow you are a fickle man,
A double-dealer and hyprocrite.
You are bold and courageous,
And at the same time,
A deceptive coward;
You are a realist
And a romantic;
And you are the *Don Juan*
Of your age,
One of a kind;
You are the one who invented
Flirtation,
And you have stolen,
Or given away,
Both the camel and its load:
You have me perplexed.

I do not mean
To confuse you

And the readers along with you;
My words only portray
My and your real condition,
My and your fancy.
I pass into various characters,
Think with their minds,
Tread with their shoes,
And take pictures of what I see.
I store it in my subconscious.
I express it in words
And watch you get confounded
At the loudness of the beats.
I rejoice and get intoxicated
With the impact the words have
In your souls,
Deep in your conscience.
You are amazed how bold they are;
You dance at their melody,
Hum their tune,
And gasp at their beauty,
For I portray you,
Portray myself;
I reveal your secret
And my own;
I draw from the depth of my being
Words that unite
And have reverberation
And rhythm.

Foreword by Bruce Ingham

In the West poetry is a somewhat unappreciated art. Most educated Englishmen can probably whistle you a few bars of Mozart or tell the difference between a Cézanne and a Picasso, but very few could recite a poem for you. In the Arab world on the other hand and in neighbouring Persia, the most generally appreciated art is in fact poetry. Particularly in Saudi Arabia, where our author comes from, and in the neighbouring Gulf States, there are two parallel strains of poetry. There is the poetry of Classical Arabic which includes poems from the pre-Islamic era up till the present day in a language which has remained unchanged as a vehicle of literary expression, just a though the Englishman of today wrote in the language of *Beowulf*. Although this poetic body has changed in content and expression it has not changed in the form of the language. There is also the tradition of the so-called Nabati, a 'Nabatean' poetry which was up till recently a purely oral one, preserving a quite archaic form of expression, literary style and content, but in the language as spoken today and very much alive in Arabian society. In this tradition even those who could not read or write could memorize, recite and compose poetry. Here a rich store of poems existed recording events from the early twentieth and nineteenth centuries and some from even earlier and being constantly added to in the modern period. These poems were the receptacle of the values and history of individual tribes and of the Arabian people in general. Famous battles and events and accounts of individual acts of generosity, nobility and bravery were enshrined in them. The body of poems included *madh* 'praise poetry', *nasiha* 'moralistic poetry', *ghazal* 'love poetry' and *hamasa* 'epic poetry' relating to specific events.

Given this tradition I doubt there are many Saudis who could not recite a few lines of either Classical or Nabatean poetry and a great many take an active interest in the art. Therefore our author is in no sense unusual in being an international businessman and also a poet. Numbers of other prominent men in Arabian society are also well known poets such as HRH Prince Khalid al-Faisal al-Saud and HE Ghazi al-Gosaibi, the present Saudi Ambassador to

London. Similarly tribal heroes of the early twentieth century, such as Rakan al Hithlain of the 'Ajman tribe, were noted poets and have well-known poems attributed to them.

The choice of subjects for these poems reflects the strong religious background of the author, his affection for his family and his interest in the political and social scene of the Middle East.

Non-Arabists will be interested, in particular, to read 'The Story of the Marriage of the Virtuous Lady to the Trustworthy Man' (pp. 17–47) which is a long poem on the early days of the prophethood of Muhammad in Arabia told from the point of view of his first wife Khadija bint al-Khuwailid. It talks of the relationship of early Islam to Judaism and Christianity, both of which were present at the time in Arabia, and reveals much of the influence of women in Arabian society.

In this poem the author talks of the various reports of the Prophet's coming circulating among Jews and Christians in Arabia at the time and of how the wealthy Khadija heard of these, having already been involved in business with Muhammad who had taken some of her camels to Damascus to sell for her there in the yearly caravan. Through various intermediaries she sends messages to him suggesting that he propose to her, which he does at the end of the poem. The verses nicely encapsulate the strong involvement of Khadija with the early days of Muhammad's prophethood.

Later poems range over politics, love, the family and the environment (p. 102):

> Wheat stalks have been persuaded
> To grow and multiply
> In stagnant water,
> And even the aunt of all,
> The palm tree,
> Has been fooled and is now watered
> By illegitimate money.

The form of the poetry is blank verse, though with sporadic temporary rhymes. Metre works over the verse rather than the line, with contrasts of long and short lines, most lines being long with the occasional short line later in the verse and some run-on lines so that the verses have a unity of rhythm and in many cases consist of one long sentence to give a parallel syntactic unity, as in (p. 11):

> You my heart, submerged
> In funloving and profligacy,
> You lead me step by step
> To climb
> To the apex of madness
> Or fall down
> To the bottom of debauchery....

The lexicon varies from poem to poem. Some, like 'The Story of the Marriage of the Virtuous Lady to the Trustworthy Man' (pp. 17–47), show the poetic literary register, while in others it is chosen from the colloquial or news media register to give a tone of stark realism. In general the poetry is philosophical and psychological rather than aesthetic and decorating, as in p. 55, talking of political solutions:

> They are all
> Like running water
> Whose clarity was sabotaged
> And objectivity spoiled
> By hypocrisy and dissemblance
> Thus becoming
> An obsolete, impossible solution,
> And indeed it is
> A terrible drug.

The poems show a range of emotions, some despairing, some bitter, some lost, some wondering. They reveal an interest in religion, but a distrust of fanaticism. Particularly in parts 6 'I? Who am I?' and 7 'You and I are Adam and Eve', they are culturally non-localized and reveal a universal character investigating aspects of identity and relationships between men and women.

School of Oriental and African Studies,
University of London
January 1996

PART ONE

To You God, My Praise and Gratitude

Praise and Gratitude to You

My belief in life and existence
Is firm.
My faith in life and mortality
Is absolute.
My faith does not blink,
Does not doubt its sanity,
Does not deviate.
It will never, never, never
Hesitate
To admit the certainty
That the end of life,
That nonexistence,
Emerges and rises
Once again
With Resurrection and Judgment.

My God, my Lord,
In the past
I committed such sins
As make my senses ashamed,
My blood curdle,
My conscience stagger,
And my skin disintegrate.
Great Forgiver and Subduer,
With Your mercy, forgive my errors,
And with Your might, vanquish my sins.

Praise Be to God

Insolent and shameless was I,
And with my insolence and shamelessness,
I blackmailed
The noble and honourable;
I was misled by the forbearance of the patient;
I felt an evil joy at seeing
The happiness of the content;
I made fun of the tolerant;
And I turned my back on scholars.
The Almighty gave me leeway,
But never forgot my doings.
I got the impression that what I did
Had no counter-effect,
No aftermath.
My sensitivity was masked,
My feelings were veiled,
And my anxiousness was pretended.
I persisted in sinning
And never admitted my ignorance;
I divorced myself from insolence and shamelessness
Only to get wed to haughtiness, malice,
And arrogance,
Fully convinced that
In everything I did
I was smart and clever.
You know what happened to me
After that.

God, the All-seeing, the Subduer knows
Who are pious and devoted
And who are debauched and dissipated;
He gives leeway but never forgets.
Glory be to Him, the Great, the Supreme.
Praise be to God,

Who alone may be praised
In adversity.

Only God Is Perfect

When I am fully awake
Or fast asleep,
When my work presses hard,
Or my dreams take me unawares,
I only settle for perfection.
My ego plays tricks,
Pretends being able
To achieve the impossible.
Every morning when I discover
How my ego has deceived me
I wake up with a headache,
And when I go back home,
Frustrated and furious
Because my thoughts have not
Reached an end,
I sprinkle misery
In every direction.
It must be that
Something is there
Which aborts my dreams;
There must be something
That frustrates my efforts.
Only after long, long suffering,
I have discovered
That sublimity and perfection
Are Yours alone.
I am only Your slave,
Son of two
Of your slaves;
My fate in Your hands;
Your judgment is incisive;
Your rulings are just.
Praise and gratitude to You.

My Memory and Question Marks

I hate my memory.
I do not want it to remember.
It is overloaded with sorrow,
And it trembles with grief.
Despair is the flag on its mast
And hopelessness is the captain of its ship.
Its crew are here and not here,
Like a fidgeting love affair,
Not knowing
Where to sail
In a sea overflowing with tears,
Swelling with sin,
And surging with atrocities.

Shall I remember? What shall I remember?
Shall I remember my overwhelming joy,
My hope for a future meeting,
Or my wishes and expectations
And the impression they have left
In my memory and my imagination?
Shall I remember my failure and my end,
The things I neglected,
Pretended to forget,
And lost
On the routes of devastation?

Shall I remember? What shall I remember?
Shall I remember that white day,
Or all the black days?
I have forgotten the colour of white.
It has changed, got soiled,
Covered by layers of dark colours.
My heart was broken when
The innocent colours of my joy
Fell into the arms of conceited hatred,

When my dreams got hooked
On error and sin,
On filthy tales and stories,
Which are like garbage
Splashed on a white gown.

Shall I remember? What shall I remember?
My crazy regret,
My buried hopes,
My anxious perplexity,
My stagnant, dormant dream,
Or my lost love,
Covered with a transparent film,
Exposed and known to everyone,
Just like a figure getting stripped in an open yard
Behind a pane of glass?
Any viewer can survey it
From A to Z.

Shall I remember? What shall I remember?
Her neck and my incantations in its sphere?
The bewitched letters,
The hand-made
Defeated words,
My poetry, resembling old, forgotten masterpieces,
And my lines and my novels,
With an amputated hand and a lost foot?
Shall I remember her chest
And the love I had in its embrace,
With numb senses,
Unmoved by body perfumes,
Unable to look at beautiful figures,
Deaf to the cries
Of any eager body?

Shall I remember? What shall I remember?
If only my memory were a sieve,
With all images seeping out;
If only I could forget,
For remembering gets me disturbed;
Remembering infuriates me;

Remembering makes me laugh
In frustration;
Remembering makes me cry
In grief.
I am a mad man remembering
What never happened
And a sane man remembering
All what happened.
I am the hero of the Arabian novel
In which a pauper marries
The sultan's daughter.

Shall I remember? What shall I remember?
When I remember,
I am unsettled and provoked
By all the question marks;
Without taking permission,
They emerge and challenge me,
While I am surrounded by confusion,
Besieged by feelings of loss,
Imprisoned in vacuum,
And buried under a pile
Of crimes and sins

Shall I remember? What shall I remember?
If only, when I remember,
I could find an answer.
If only my fate, my soul –
If only dispersal would know my lot;
If only my looks and my steps
Knew the way to the door;
If only devils and demons,
And magicians lurking
In Satan's lap,
Got an answer.

Shall I remember? What shall I remember?
When I remember
Question marks bite me.
But still
Do not wonder and do not swear;

You will not miss watching
My affliction and sleeplessness.
Wait! Do wait;
The end is close,
And I, at the beginning and at the end,
Yield myself to God
And choose to be driven
By the Merciful.
In my mind, there is a sura
On mercy and forgiveness,
And in my conviction, a verse
Which speaks of clemency:
'Say, "O servants of God, you that have sinned
Against your souls,
Do not despair of God's mercy,
For He forgives all sins.
He is the Forgiving One, the Merciful." '

It Is by the Remembrance of God

You my heart, submerged
In playfulness and buffoonery,
Avoiding confrontation
By hiding and evasion,
Paying no attention to
The final act,
The conclusion,
Being preoccupied with silk daydreams
You yourself weave ...

You my heart, crushed
By funloving and profligacy,
Sunken into a sea
Of doubts and suspicions,
That has no beginning and no end,
No center and no bottom ...

You my heart, submerged
In funloving and profligacy,
You lead me step by step
To climb
To the apex of madness
Or fall down
To the bottom of debauchery ...

And you,
My prone-to-evil soul,
You distract me
With the wand of pleasure,
You set me on fire
With the whips of desire;
My senses burn,
And my body roars,
So I rush fast
On torture road.

You, my soul,
Content with the explicitness of falsehood,
You make evil tempting,
Permit the forbidden,
And forbid the permissible;
I end up with all my being
Overtaken by colocynth.

You, my soul,
Are my consort,
My devil.
I keep asking again and again,
How should I deal with you?
How can I explore you?
How do I handle you?

And you, my brain,
You are undoubtedly upset,
Confused, and unsettled;
You have reached
No decision yet.

As for you, my heart –
Here I come back to you –
You are dreaming, fast asleep;
You are hooked, and infatuated.
Hooked on an illusion
And infatuated with a lurking square,
Which has taken hold of
My house and my land,
My shadow and my shade,
From north to south
And from east to west.

You, my mind,
Wake up, beware
Go free and free me
From my consort, my devil.
Give me orders;
Impress your communiqués
Into my veins

So that they may
Run into my blood,
Forcing me not to forget:
To remember God and contemplate,
For only with the remembrance of God

My hearts are reassured
And my mind clear up,
There is no God but You,
And no Mercy but comes from You.

PART TWO

I Love You, I Love You, I Love You! Beloved Messenger of God

Story of the Marriage of the Virtuous Lady and the Trustworthy Man

Let us begin
By praying for peace to be –
Upon God's beloved,
Messenger of the Lord of creation
And the one all believers love.
Peace, blessings and benediction be
Upon you and upon your kin,
Other prophets, your Companions,
And the pious and righteous,
Whether your contemporaries
Or later followers.
O most noble of all creatures and of all messengers,
O God's means of mercy for all creation,
God's prophet, God's messenger,
Peace, blessings and benediction be
Upon you, my beloved master,
Muhammad, son of Abdullah.
I love you, I love you, I love you!
I love whomever you love,
Whatever you love,
And whoever loves you,
Beloved messenger of God.

I pray for peace, blessings and benediction
To be upon the first person to believe
In the long awaited, chosen man.
She was a distinguished woman
Of great esteem and noble lineage,
Singular and honourable,
Wealthy and eminent;
A woman of keen insight,
Of tolerance and wisdom.
She is a Mistress of Women in Paradise;

The mother of radiant Fatima,
The prophet's daughter,
And another Mistress of Paradise Women;
And the mother of all his other daughters.
She is the pure and chaste
Khadija, daughter of Khwailed,
Whose brother was married to Safia,
An aunt of Prophet
Muhammed Ibn Abdullah.
I love you, I love you, I love you!
I love whomever you love,
Whatever you love,
And whoever loves you,
Beloved messenger of God.

His uncle Abu Taleb addressed him one day,
Exhorting him,
'It is now time, Muhammad,
For your tribe's camels
To set off for Syria,
And Khadija Bint Khwailed
Sends some of our tribesmen
To trade for her.
Thus they make some profit for themselves.
If you go to her
And offer your services,
She would take you right away,
Preferring you to others,
For what she would certainly learn
Of your honesty.'
Curtly and with self respect,
The proud young man retorted,
'Let her send for me, then,'
And turned around and left.
I love you, I love you, I love you!
I love whomever you love,
Whatever you love,
And whoever loves you,
Beloved messenger of God.

His Aunt Atikah was present

And followed the conversation.
She went to the chaste lady
And told her the gist
Of what went between
The honest young man and his uncle
At their house.
'I thought he had his chance
In the Hashem trade,'
The chaste lady commented.
She sent for him,
And he headed for her house,
With his fast strides
And flowing limbs.
I love you, I love you, I love you!
I love whomever you love,
Whatever you love,
And whoever loves you,
Beloved messenger of God.

She received him with warmth
And greeted him with respect.
She was twenty seven.
She had a bright forehead
And was beautiful, like spring.
Her eyes had a gleam
Which knew where to go,
A gleam that lit her way,
A gleam that suggested alertness and intelligence.
For no clear reason,
She felt hopeful and happy,
Reassured and relieved.
He was twenty five.
He had dark, large eyes,
Strong hands and feet,
Broad shoulders,
And thick hair reaching his ear lobes.
His front teeth had a gap in between,
And his complexion was reddish.
Over his shoulder lurked a great secret.
When he gestured, he used his whole hand.
When he expressed wonder,

He turned it up and down,
And when glad,
He lowered his glance.
His most extreme laugh was a smile.
His speech was articulate
And his manners perfect.
I love you, I love you, I love you!
I love whomever you love,
Whatever you love,
And whoever loves you,
Beloved messenger of God.

His words enchanted her,
And his dignity overwhelmed her.
Her senses were captivated
By his pride and shyness.
She felt she was talking
To the ideal man,
A man different from all the nobility
And all the chiefs
Of Quraysh, their tribe.
'I shall give you,' she said,
'Twice as much as I usually offer
Any of your tribesmen.
It is because of what I have learned
Of your telling the truth,
Your great honesty,
And your noble personality.'
He left her dazzled,
Spellbound;
His voice, sweet, firm and enchanting,
Still ringing in her ears.
She wondered in retrospect
How he never looked fully at her;
He talked to her with his eyes down.
She felt greatly exalted,
Thinking of this noble-mannered Hashemite
Who had filled her heart with splendour
And, by God's grace, made her hours
Pass in content and happiness,
In joy and comfort.

I love you, I love you, I love you!
I love whomever you love,
Whatever you love,
And whoever loves you,
Beloved messenger of God.

His first mission of trade
For Khwailed's daughter
Was to the Habarisha market place,
The largest in Tihama.
When the caravan returned,
Khadija was anxious
To talk to her servant, Mayssara,
Who had accompanied the trustworthy man.
'But why am I so anxious and worried?
How often have I listened
To Mayssara and his trade news,
Tidings of loss and gain;
What is it this time
That makes me so anxious?'
After extensive talk,
Full of news of her trade,
The boy sensed that she wanted
Him to tell her
About the young Hashemite.
He felt that her satisfaction
Would be in listening
To sweet news about him.
So Mayssara told her
How the young man was
A most honest merchant,
Who never swore,
Nor raised his voice;
How he was proud but never cruel;
How he was a match for the greatest misfortune
And the heaviest burden.
How when he talked,
He won the hearts of his listeners,
And when he said something,
It was the final word;
How he never cheated or deceived his customers,

And when his merchandise had any flaw,
He pointed it out;
How he was a truly trustworthy man.
As she listened to her servant,
Her heart overflowed with bliss,
Hope covered all her soul,
And a song stirred in her breast.
I love you, I love you, I love you!
I love whomever you love,
Whatever you love,
And whoever loves you,
Beloved messenger of God.

His second trip
Was decisive and full of events.
He was at the head of a caravan
As great as all the other caravans
Of the Hashem tribe,
With all its clans.
And his intimate friend,
Abu Bakr, the Truthful Man,
Was with the caravan of his folks,
Which pleased Muhammad, the chosen one.
Before departure, Mayssara,
As was his habit,
Went to his mistress,
To listen to her instructions
And recommendations.
Honourable Khadija told him,
'Never cross Muhammad
Or disobey him.'
I love you, I love you, I love you!
I love whomever you love,
Whatever you love,
And whoever loves you,
Beloved messenger of God.

Caravans tire and must stop to rest,
Then with renewed vigour
Resume their journey
And cover great distances.

Days pass
And evenings are the time
For relaxation and pleasant chats.
That's how it went on this occasion,
Until one day Busra, in Syria,
Could be seen from a distance,
And the caravans came to a halt
To catch their breath,
Get new supplies,
And check their merchandise.
They camped at a spot
Close to the hermitage of Nestora
The hermit.
The two friends
Muhammad and Abu Bakr
Sat in the shade of a tree.
Abu Bakr took his leave to run some errand,
Leaving Muhammad alone under the tree.
The hermit was going around
In the caravan camp,
Studying the faces
And trying to explore the souls.
All of a sudden he caught sight
Of Muhammad, the man he was looking for.
He saw a handsome young man
Of a radiant complexion,
A great man of noble origin,
With Arabian features,
Of medium height
And with a large head,
A wide forehead,
A long beard,
A broad chest
A long neck
And thick hands and feet.
His head was topped
With thick, pitch black hair,
And his large black eyes
Shone with appeal and attraction
Under long, dark eyelashes
I love you, I love you, I love you!

I love whomever you love,
Whatever you love,
And whoever loves you,
Beloved messenger of God.

'He must be the awaited prophet,
Of whom earlier prophets foretold,'
Said the hermit to himself
Again and again.
He came across Mayssara,
Who knew the young man well.
The hermit inquired,
'Who is that, there under the tree?'
'A man of Quraysh,'
Answered Mayssara,
'Of those in charge of the Holy Place.'
'Is there always some red colour in his eyes?'
'Yes, always,' replied Mayssara.
The hermit rushed down
To where the awaited prophet was sitting.
'I implore you by Lat and Izza, what is your name?'
The young man's face clouded, and he said,
'Leave me alone!'
The hermit knew this was a man
Who hated idols and deities.
He apologized
And kept asking questions
With great interest.
The young man answered.
As the hermit finally rose, he said,
'Muhammad, I can find in you
All the evidence and all
Except one sign,
Which I couldn't spot.
Would you uncover your shoulder?'
The chosen one did,
And there it was,
The seal of prophethood,
Shining in its right place.
The hermit, in great awe,
Embraced and kissed him.

I love you, I love you, I love you!
I love whomever you love,
Whatever you love,
And whoever loves you,
Beloved messenger of God.

The hermit climbed back
To his hermitage
And looked at the people down.
He was holding a sheet in his hand.
Shaking it, he addressed them,
'Hey everybody!
I swear by Him who erected the skies
Without pillars
That in this sheet it is told
That the man sitting down there
Under that tree
Is a messenger of the Lord of Creation.
God will send him
With an unsheathed sword
And with the greatest gain.
Whoever follows him is saved,
And whoever disobey him goes astray.'
The hermit's voice rang deep
Inside Abu Bakr's heart
And in Mayssara's ears.
The rest went about their business,
With indifference to what was said.
I love you, I love you, I love you!
I love whomever you love,
Whatever you love,
And whoever loves you,
Beloved messenger of God.

The caravans arrived in Syria.
Stalls were erected,
And the people of Quraysh,
Who dwelt in the neighborhood of the Sacred House,
Sold and bought
In that summer trip of theirs.
When the market was over

And it was time for goodbyes,
The caravans prepared for the trip
Back home to the Ancient House.
Days passed with them on the road,
With great events looming in the horizon,
Until they arrived at the Dhahran pass
Between Makkah and Asfan.
Here Mayssara asked Muhammad
To go ahead of the caravan
And tell Khadija what befell her trade
By the grace of God.
When she saw the trustworthy one,
Khadija was swept by yearning.
She couldn't really tell what came over her.
He went ahead to tell her
How their profit was twice as much
As they used to make.
But she did not care for profit.
She asked,
'Muhammad, where is Mayssara?'
'I left him back in the desert,'
He answered simply.
Promptly she retorted,
'Go in haste to him;
Let him come here as fast as he can.'
She was anxious and unsettled,
Desiring to hear from her servant
What Muhammad did on the trip.
She had a feeling that he will have
A great status
In her life and in history.
I love you, I love you, I love you!
I love whomever you love,
Whatever you love,
And whoever loves you,
Beloved messenger of God.

When Mayssara had related
The whole hermit episode
Khwailed's daughter
Went to her cousin Waraqa

And told him what she had heard from Mayssara.
Waraqa Ibn Nofal said,
'If this is true, Khadija,
Muhammad must be the nation's prophet.
I have known a prophet of this nation is due,
And this is the right timing.'
I love you, I love you, I love you!
I love whomever you love,
Whatever you love,
And whoever loves you,
Beloved messenger of God.

He was over twenty and not yet married.
Al-Abbas, Hamza, and Abu Bakr –
All got married.
What was it that kept Abdullah's son
From getting married?
Was it that he was short of money?
Who would have rejected him
When he was a man of noble birth,
Honour, purity, and honesty?
All high moral standards were his.
The nobility and prominent figures
Of the Hashem clan,
As well as the clans of Umayya, Tamim,
Asad, and Makhzoum,
Would have been pleased and joyful
Beyond any measure
Were the trustworthy young man
To propose to one of their daughters.
All their girls, with no exception,
Dreamt of him.
But Muhammad Ibn Abdullah
Was beginning to feel
That transcendence, sublimation
In the prime spot of God's universe
Were better than the whole world
And everything in it.
I love you, I love you, I love you!
I love whomever you love,
Whatever you love,

And whoever loves you,
Beloved messenger of God.

When night enveloped Makkah
Ladies of the noble families
Of Quraysh and the other clans
Used to take advantage of the dark
To visit the Ancient House
And circle around the Ka'aba.
Khadija Bint Khwailed
Used to make the circles with others
Feeling satisfied
With the profit she made in trade.
Never complaining or opening up to anyone,
Other than One and Only,
About the difficulties and troubles
Of her marriages.
She remembered now
How she used to wait,
Or arrange, for the chance
To listen to her cousin
Waraqa Ibn Nofal
Talking of religion and prophets
And telling stories
Of ancient nations and cultures.
She also remembered
Her two marriages.
She had married 'Atiq of the Makhzoum clan
Before she was fifteen.
She wanted so badly for her husband
To be distinguished among men,
But death snatched him from her.
She married next a man
Called Hind Ibn Zarara,
And they had two daughters,
Hala and Hind.
But it was a brief marriage;
Her husband's aspirations
Couldn't rise to the level of hers,
So she left him.
Thus this prominent lady of Quraysh,

Known as the Virtuous Lady,
Was left without a spouse or a mate
Even before she was twenty five.
As she circled the Ancient House,
She continued to remember
Details of her life,
And at the end of her circumambulation,
She recalled what her cousin
Had told her about the Trustworthy young man.
She kept repeating the words
Aloud and to herself:
'If this is true, Khadija,
Muhammad must be this nation's prophet.
I have known a prophet of this nation is due,
And this is the right timing.'
I love you, I love you, I love you!
I love whomever you love,
Whatever you love,
And whoever loves you,
Beloved messenger of God.

Having finished her circling,
She headed home,
And gone to bed,
Khadija fell fast asleep.
In her dream she saw
A great sun landing in her house
Filling it with light,
Which overflowed
To cover all places and all countries,
Dazzling the souls, hearts, and minds
Of people,
After dazzling their eyes.
She work up trembling and terrified.
When she had calmed down,
She wanted to go back to sleep,
But it deserted her eyes.
Her mind was wide awake
And her heart disturbed.
She thought the matter over.
Here were her mind and her heart;

The one did not stop thinking,
And the other kept on beating fast.
Her common sense failed her,
And she shouldn't make things out.
When morning came
She hastened to her cousin,
The righteous Waraqa Ibn Nofal
And found him absorbed in reading.
When her voice reached his ears,
He looked up in astonishment.
'The Virtuous Lady?
What brings you here
At this hour?'
She told him her dream,
And cheerfully and, affectionately he told her,
'Rejoice, cousin!
If your dream comes true,
The light of prophethood
Will dwell in your house,
And out of that house,
The radiance of the last prophet
Will overflow.
I love you, I love you, I love you!
I love whomever you love,
Whatever you love,
And whoever loves you,
Beloved messenger of God.

Quraysh women had a special feast,
On which they would meet at the Sacred House.
On the day of the feast, the Virtuous Lady,
Dressed in silk
And accompanied by her maids,
Joined them, entering through Abraham's Gate.
She circumambulated the Ancient House
And stopped to pray.
She asked God for a great thing,
Not related to her trade or wealth;
She prayed for her dream to come true.
After circling, all the women
Sat down to partake

Of the feast meal,
When all of a sudden a Jew shouted,
'Women of Quraysh,
A prophet will soon appear in your tribe,
His time is near.
Any woman who has the chance
To be his wife
Should do so.'
I love you, I love you, I love you!
I love whomever you love,
Whatever you love,
And whoever loves you,
Beloved messenger of God.

The Virtuous Lady went back
To her castle, her house,
Her soul delving deep
Into recent events:
Her dream, which was so real,
Coming after Mayssara's words
About the hermit, Muhammad, and prophethood,
And what she was told by her cousin.
The Jew's voice was still ringing in her ears.
She felt an overwhelming desire
To confide in him,
Tell him what she felt in her heart.
She told herself,
'I do not want to flirt with him;
I am the most eminent lady of Quraysh
And I am honorable and virtuous.
All I want is to talk to him,
Give him an encouraging hint
To propose to me.'
She acted fast;
She sent for him.
He asked for his uncle's permission
And headed for her house.
As soon as he got there,
She came to meet him,
Feeling confused and unsteady.
She took his noble hand

And held it to her breast
And upper chest.
She said, 'Believe you me,
I would never do such a thing,
Except that I hope you are
The awaited prophet.
If you are,
I know my place and my right,
And I can pray to God
Who will send you to me.'
The honest young man answered,
'If I am him,
You have done for me
What I will never forget,
And if it is someone else,
Then God, for whom you are doing this,
Will never forget you.'
I love you, I love you, I love you!
I love whomever you love,
Whatever you love,
And whoever loves you,
Beloved messenger of God.

Hala, daughter of Khwailed
Asked Ammar Ibn Yasser,
One of the Makhzoum clan slaves,
'Wouldn't your friend like
To marry Khadija?'
Ammar hastened to his honest, discreet friend,
'Would you be interested
In marrying Khadija Bint Khwailed?'
The heart beat of the trustworthy young man
Went faster
And with a smile on his lips,
He said, 'Indeed I would.'
Hala went back to her sister
With the good news.
On the following day,
The virtuous lady waited
For the honest young man
To come and propose.

Time passed as slowly as it does
When one is on a tiring journey,
Covering long distances.
So she sent him a friend of hers
To ask him what keeps him
From getting married.
He answered, 'I cannot afford it.'
When Khadija's friend said,
'What would you say if you were spared
All expenses and invited to marry
A lady of nobility, wealth, and beauty?'
He asked 'Who is that?'
'Khadija Bint Khwailed,' she replied.
He asked again, 'How can that be?'
'Let me take care of it,' she said.
The delighted friend went back to Khadija
With the good news.
I love you, I love you, I love you!
I love whomever you love,
Whatever you love,
And whoever loves you,
Beloved messenger of God.

She said softly to one of her maids,
'Go to him.
Ask him to come here at once.'
When he arrived she said,
'Aren't you going to get married, Muhammad?'
'Whom?' he asked.
She said, 'Me!'
'How would you marry me,' he replied,
'When you are Quraysh's wealthy widow
And I am only her orphan boy?'
'Well, cousin,
What attracts me to you
Is your kinship, your position among your people,
Your honesty and high moral standards,
And your truthfulness.
Go to your uncle,
And ask him to come here quickly.'
When he was back with his uncle,

She addressed the old man.
'Go to my uncle and propose
For your nephew to marry me.'
Abd Al-Muttaleb's son answered,
'Don't make fun of us, Khadija.'
'This is God's doing,'
She said excitedly.
I love you, I love you, I love you!
I love whomever you love,
Whatever you love,
And whoever loves you,
Beloved messenger of God.

'People of Quraysh, be my witnesses;
I am giving Khadija Bint Khwailed
In marriage
To Muhammad Ibn Abdullah.'
This was the announcement
Of her uncle, Amr Ibn Asad.
The poor young man slaughtered two camels
For people to feast on,
And Khadija ordered her maids
To sing and dance,
For this was for her the end
Of days of yearning and frustration.
The happy Abu Taleb commented,
'Something great will happen to this pair.'
The Sun did land in the house
And so began the journey
Of the well-guided man
On the righteous path,
And light overflowed to cover
All creation
At the hands of God's messenger,
Muhammad, the truthful and trustworthy,
The man with noble manners,
Full of mercy and tenderness
For the faithful,
God's means of mercy for all creation
My beloved master
And master of all creatures

God's beloved prophet,
And the one all believers love
Wherever they belong.
I love you, I love you, I love you!
I love whomever you love,
Whatever you love,
And whoever loves you,
Beloved messenger of God.

How Much Do I Love You, Darling

Every day, without failing,
Ever since she has learned to write,
My little girl Amina
Leaves for me, on my pillow,
A piece of paper
Perfumed with love and innocence,
With which I take off the clothes of my toil and strife.
She cheers me up with her note
And waters the seed of my happiness,
Turning it every night
Into a shady tree with many branches.

Once she wrote,
'I love you, daddy,
Because you taught me how to pray.
When I used to go to bed,
I had dreams of an evil boy
And of jinni and demons,
But since I have started to pray
The Isha and the even and odd prayers
I dream of angels.'
How much do I love you, darling?
My love is as vast as the sea,
As great as the number of sea waves,
And to you I dedicate
All the words
That express love.

You are Amina;
You hold the same name as my mother,
And as the woman who bore and gave birth to
God's beloved messenger.
I love him, I love him, I love him!
I love whomever he loves,
Whatever he loves,

*And whoever loves him,
Beloved messenger of God.*

I Love You, First, Second, and Third

Your anniversary, beloved,
Your birthday comes
Year after year,
And I will never hesitate
To express my feeling,
Whether I am at home
Among my folks and my children,
In my mansion
Among my mates and dear friends,
Or in my tomb,
There, close to your grave,
My beloved, my neighbor, the messenger I believe in,
I love you, I love you, I love you!
I love whomever you love,
Whatever you love,
And whoever loves you,
Beloved messenger of God.

When I remember my children,
My folks, and my dear friends,
I also recall your birthday, beloved,
The day on which the devil mourned
And felt miserable,
While the universe rejoiced
And all creatures joined in a dance,
I forget everybody
And remember you, beloved;
I remember your birthday, beloved,
For I love you, first, beloved,
And I love you, second, beloved,
And I love you, third, beloved,
And my love expands and continues
Forever,
My beloved, my neighbor, the messenger I believe in,
I love you, I love you, I love you!

I love whomever you love,
Whatever you love,
And whoever loves you,
Beloved messenger of God.

My children and my folks,
My own flesh and blood,
Veins of my heart
And blood vessels of my being,
My genes, my atoms,
My hopes and aspirations,
My sighs and tears,
My joys and smiles,
My pride and glory,
My torches and candles,
Screams that are suppressed
Deep inside me,
My living failures,
My lasting victories,
My forgotten sorrows,
My continuous celebrations,
My plants and my harvest,
My friends and relatives,
My daughters and sons –
You are all in the smaller scale,
And you, beloved,
Are all alone
In the heavier, larger one.
I love you, I love you, I love you!
I love whomever you love,
Whatever you love,
And whoever loves you,
Beloved messenger of God.

My own flesh and blood,
I can only praise you
And love you,
But only through my love,
To him who is my shield
And my protection,
The crown on my head.

I will sing a song of love to him,
And then I will sing to them,
One by one.
I love you, I love you, I love you!
I love whomever you love,
Whatever you love,
And whoever loves you,
Beloved messenger of God.

What I want to tell you,
Sons and daughters of mine,
Is that when I remember you,
When I praise you,
And when I love you,
I think of him.
And when I chose your names,
I was thinking of him.
It is your good fortune
That you are connected to my beloved,
By virtue of kinship
And by virtue of religion and intercession.
It is a lasting connection
Which has melted into
A sublime, spiritual love,
That has left the earth
To soar high
And gain the world of immortality.
My love will speed over distances
And shorten time
To get to you, beloved.
My beloved, my neighbor, the messenger I believe in,
I love you, I love you, I love you!
I love whomever you love,
Whatever you love,
And whoever loves you,
Beloved messenger of God.

My own flesh and blood,
I will mention you, praise you,
And sing my love to you,
One at a time,

Beginning with the one
Who comes to my mind first.
It is you, Muhammad,
Whom I think of first.
Well, Muhammad, Muhammad –
Sorry, my master and beloved,
How could my spontaneity
Make me forget propriety and good manners
And thus write your name
Without writing first
'My beloved,' 'master,' or 'lord'?
And how could I address you
In the singular form
When you are everybody?
For I named you after
The lord of all Adam's children,
My beloved and also God's beloved,
The noblest child born to a woman,
My master and lord, God's messenger!
I love you, I love you, I love you!
I love whomever you love,
Whatever you love,
And whoever loves you,
Beloved messenger of God.

Of course, beloved, I love you:
I love your long face,
Your bright, intense black eyes,
Your radiant joy,
Your round frown,
Your rare pessimism
And frequent optimism.
I love everything about you.
You have been wise
Since you have known God.
Because you love God,
I will not worry about you
Or worry because of you
Ever, ever,
My beloved Muhammad.
I love you, I love you, I love you!

I love whomever you love,
Whatever you love,
And whoever loves you,
Beloved messenger of God.

One day they brought me the tidings
That I am the father of a baby girl;
I thanked God
And decided to choose for her
An Arabic name, never used by Arabs before
Throughout their history.
I uttered the call for prayer in her ear
And said, 'God has named you
Rotana,
Most delicious date fruit
Of the most beautiful palm tree,
One of the palms of the beloved city,
Madina, the Radiant.
You are honey to my taste,
And in my heart, a spring;
You are the source of my happiness,
The pasture of my smiles,
And a neighbor of my beloved,
My master and lord, God's messenger!
I love you, I love you, I love you!
I love whomever you love,
Whatever you love,
And whoever loves you,
Beloved messenger of God.

You Dalia,
My eldest daughter,
I nursed you with my own hands
Pure milk
From my soul and heart.
I often stayed up late with you,
And enjoyed your company to a great extent.
It was you who dispelled
The heaps of misery I was under
And the vacuum I had experienced.
I took you

On a trip of light
To the Mosque of the Prophet
Who will intercede for all Muslims.
There, I embraced you before his tomb
And prayed for peace and blessing for him.
And prayed God to give you and me
The chance to take a sip
From the Fount of Abundance
Out of his own noble hand.
It would be a drink after which
We should never feel thirsty.
I love you, I love you, I love you!
I love whomever you love,
Whatever you love,
And whoever loves you,
Beloved messenger of God.

Fatima,
Girl with the most beautiful name,
When in your sphere,
I am in the sweetest environment.
You are my wish and my hope.
On account of your namesake,
The beloved chosen one
Got very angry.
He went up his rostrum
Because Ali, her husband,
Considered taking another wife,
Which would have angered her.
And I would never, ever accept
For your husband
To have another wife.
In this, I follow
The example of the beloved
Messenger of God.
I hate what he hates
And loves what he loves.
I am pleased with what pleased him
And infuriated with what infuriated him.
I love you, I love you, I love you!
I love whomever you love,

Whatever you love,
And whoever loves you,
Beloved messenger of God.

And you Amina,
My love for you is two-fold:
My love for you
As my flesh and blood,
And my love for my mother,
After whom I named you.
My mother was named by my grandfather
After the virtuous mother
Of my beloved lord and master,
The lord of all creatures
And human beings.
I love you, I love you, I love you!
I love whomever you love,
Whatever you love,
And whoever loves you,
Beloved messenger of God.

First I wanted to call you Khadija,
After the first person to believe
In the black-eyed prophet,
The most handsome of God's creatures
And closest to perfection.
He was sent to be
God's mercy to all creation
And the intercessor for unquestioning Muslims,
The beloved messenger of God.
But my affection for my beloved wife,
Your mother, Nasiba,
And my reverence and respect
For the heroic Partisan Nasiba
Who offered her life as a sacrifice
To save the lord of all creatures
On the day of the Uhud battle,
Made me decide to name you Nasiba.
So, beloved Nasiba,
You are close to my heart,
Which nursed you.

You often make me confused
Whether you are your mother
Or your mother is you.
You have made me certain
That I am a unique person,
With two hearts,
Which beat and overflow
With love for the two of you.
Time will never again be as generous
And give anyone else
Two persons like you two.
For me you are like the two suns,
Al-Hassan and Al-Hussein,
The two grandsons of my lord,
God's messenger.
I love you, I love you, I love you!
I love whomever you love,
Whatever you love,
And whoever loves you,
Beloved messenger of God.

And as for you Arwa,
You are my pet,
My money box and my harvest.
You are my gold and my silver!
You are all my gems and my whole wealth!
I am proud of you
Because you are wise;
In the daytime you are hardworking and efficient
And you spend the night praying.
You are destined
To have strong faith and be eminent.
I only hope that you will be
Like your aunt,
The noble Arwa,
Aunt of the beloved messenger of God.
I love you, I love you, I love you!
I love whomever you love,
Whatever you love,
And whoever loves you,
Beloved messenger of God.

My first son, Qaswara,
You have been given this name
By your grandfather
So that you would be
The first Arab male
Named Qaswara.
You are a stubborn lion,
And you are the distinguished chosen one,
The dear one.
Your immediate grandfather Ali
Is a grandson of Al-Hussein,
The martyred son of radiant Fatima,
While your remote grandfather Ali
Was a cousin of God's messenger.
I was told by my father
That he wanted to call you Hamza,
But he opted for Qaswara,
So, by the Grace of God,
You will be another lighthouse,
As was Hamza, your uncle,
And the uncle of God's prophet.
I love you, I love you, I love you!
I love whomever you love,
Whatever you love,
And whoever loves you,
Beloved messenger of God.

Sons and daughters
I urge you to love your grandfather,
The man I love and God Himself loves,
More than you love yourselves,
Your mother, or me.
Parents and grandparents
Urge upon their children
That through loving the beloved messenger,
One and one's parents are saved
From Hell and fire.
It is a source of strength
And sustenance
In this mortal life
And the everlasting Hereafter.

My beloved one, you are the interceder
For the submissive pious,
For passionate lovers,
And for the trembling infatuate.
You are a bright light,
Dear beloved,
The shining, lasting moon,
With which God,
Glory be to Him,
Sheds light on the whole world,
From the six days of its creation
To the moment of its vanishing,
The Hour of Resurrection.
You are, dear beloved, the mercy
God, the Merciful, has extended
To mankind.
As the Compassionate and Merciful,
The True and Just,
Has described you,
You are kind and merciful
To all believers.
It is from your noble hand,
Dear beloved,
That we will receive a drink,
After which we will never be thirsty.
My beloved and God's beloved,
My beloved and God's prophet.
I love you, I love you, I love you!
I love whomever you love,
Whatever you love,
And whoever loves you,
Beloved messenger of God.

PART THREE

People, Listen and Comprehend

A Lentil Soup River

Folks, people,
Listen and comprehend, or do not comprehend!
Close your eyes,
And utter not a word;
The Sultan is getting a surprise
Prepared for you
In the form of a gift.
Accept it without hesitation,
Without discussion,
And thank the Sultan
For his gift.

Folks, people,
The Sultan's gift is a surprise,
How many times we have said and repeated –
Perhaps a thousand times –
That it is not any merchandise
Or cash.
It is something similar to an animal,
Some brother of the buffalo.
It is certainly a creature
With a soul.

Folks, people,
Undoubtedly you know the bogey,
Who devours and babbles,
Who ordered you about
Without making orders,
Who used to eat
The banana and its peel,
Fat animals and skinny,
And to imprison in the Sultan's jail
Those who go to bed early
And those who stay up.

Folks, people,
I can tell what's in your minds,
What you feel at heart,
And what goes on in your brains.
I know that you are acting
And that you do not know
Whom the Sultan means.
You insist
That every single person
In the Sultan's government
Is a bogey,
That every guard
Of the Sultan's chair
Is a bogey,
That every relative of a person
In the Sultan's government
Is a bogey,
And that every friend
Of a person who guards
The Sultan's chair
Is a bogey,
That everybody is a bogey
And everybody
Devours and babbles.

Folks, people,
I will give a sign.
It won't be a phrase,
Nor a lighthouse.
The strong man, the Sultan,
Means something,
Which is neither a beast nor a human being,
Nor does he mean an atheist or a religious leader,
And certainly he does not mean
Adel Imam.[1]

Folks, people,
Do you know the bogey
Who throws into jail

---

[1] A famous movie star.

Grapes and watermelons?
Who finds entertainment
In killing people
With acid and arsenic?
Who has ordered that
A lentil soup river
Should flow into
The Lake of Spinach?
Who forces you to use
Doughnuts for money,
And to take off your gowns
And wear nothing but
Socks and neckties?

Folks, people,
Have you realized after all the clues
I have so far given you
That the Sultan
Wants to remove your anxiety,
Apprehension and sleeplessness?
That he wants you to enjoy
Sound sleep
And to be sure
That what has happened
Was not ordered by the Sultan,
Even if people say
And prove
That every thing that has taken place
And will take place
Is ordered by the Sultan?

No Way out Without Blood

Tyrants are only made
By ignoble people and slaves,
While freedom roses can only bloom
When watered with a holy mixture
Of the perfume of truth
And a magic drinking oil
Which springs out of the heart
Of honesty and justice
And flows through the furious
And combat-ready
Arteries and veins
To reach the brain,
Where flaming banners are flown,
With the constitution of liberty
Inscribed on them.
Through struggle and resistance,
Determination and fighting,
These banners declare
That men, women, and children
Are the oil, the fuel,
And that blood
Is the medicine which will ease
The pains of slavery
And will fly
The standards of freedom

As for stupid solutions,
Like using entente for a cover,
And like cheek kissing
And embraces,
While the sincerity of hearts
Is under doubt,
And like taking shelter
Under a steel canopy
Instead of the stupid, worn-out curtain –

They are all
Like running water
Whose clarity was sabotaged
And objectivity spoiled
By hypocrisy and dissemblance,
Thus becoming
An obsolete, impossible solution,
And indeed it is
A terrible drug.

Those terrible drugs of domination –
How many leaders and rulers
They have intoxicated,
Drugged,
And hooked,
And once they are addicted, they find
Peaceful methods too restrictive,
And through promotion,
Clamour, and proclamation,
Dormant hatreds
And forgotten bitterness
Are awakened.
Therefore, today,
There is no solution, no escape,
No road to take,
No relief from hardship,
No door,
No window,
And no way out
Without blood.

The Fire Under the Ashes Burn All!

'I see under the ashes,
The sparkle of fire.'
Between the words I hear
Phrases like firebrands.
As for the tape,
Its cover has
A radiant gleam,
While inside it, fire breaks out,
Coming from all directions
The trend of violence and fanaticism,
The supporters of parties and party feuds,
And the team of reckless saboteurs,
And there on paper
There is a small influential group
Of hypocrites
And a small lost group
Of moderates,
While the terrified majority
Insist on feeling nothing,
Seeing nothing,
Hearing nothing,
Or they believe
That taking one side
Will cause trouble,
Raise a question
About *issues*,
Bring a charge
Of falsification of facts,
And cause fear
Of false accusations.
Everybody hides behind a wall
Which is full of holes,
Exposing what should be covered
And allowing voices and whispers
To be heard.

Everybody is inattentive and believes
That he is full of self control
And is invulnerable,
That his secret is safe
And undisturbed.
No one has comprehended
Or realized
That they all are under ashes,
And under the ashes
A fire is burning.

It Bit My Hand!

A starving *dog* followed me,
Walking on four.
I tried to get rid of it,
But could not.
It pained me to see
How skinny it was,
And I couldn't sleep,
Thinking of its abjectness
And its barking.
Its homelessness distressed me,
So I took it to my castle,
I cleaned and fed it
And allowed it to get warm.
I gave it the task
Of guarding my supplies.
It became my companion
And one of my mates.
It had the impression
That it knew all my secrets,
My whole life story,
My camping sites, my playgrounds,
And my arsenals.
I failed to realize that it suffers
From meanness and ingratitude.
And so it bit my hand,
The same hand
That gave it food.

I am warning you
That the *dog*, which you take
For a faithful animal
May turn into a human monster,
Walking on two.
That is exactly
How it went:

The *dog* I fed
Bit my hand
And stole two of my vehicles.
It loaded one
With some supplies of mine
And carried on the other
Part of my arsenal.
About my private life,
It made up many stories,
And turned my biography
Into tall tales,
Forgetting to remember
What it knew
About me:
That I do not sleep,
I will not sleep,
I never sleep.

The Forbidden Food Banquet

In every terrified country,
Among every trembling nation,
In every land which is submissive
Even to the slaughterer's knife,
Among every yellow
Cowardly, backward people,
There is a common
Single rule,
A clear, unmistakble sign;
It is terror.
Terror is a two-way street.
The people and the whole land,
Are afraid;
They fear the authorities,
The self appointed rulers,
And the sultan.
The government and its systems
Of security and intelligence,
The armies of detectives,
And the prison wardens
Are all afraid;
They fear the people and public opinion,
And they fear organizations and liberty.

A believer fears nothing
But God,
And a believing righteous regime fears nothing
But God.
Cowardice and backwardness
Only spread and multiply
In an infidel land
Among the ingrate
Who do not appreciate God's blessings
Or among a nation of atheists
And unbelieving rulers.

There, all the multitudes
Have a common denominator,
Which is unbelief in God.
And there
Everyone has taken an oath
To be a contestant
In a competition
Of debauchery and dissipation,
Of executing freedom,
And of flying,
The banners of lechery.

As for me, you, he, and she
Within the borders
And outside,
Each of us is only a guest
Or the host
Of a banquet
Of forbidden food
Inside a lofty palace
With an exterior of marble,
An interior of grime,
And mean owners.

PART FOUR

Philosophical Thoughts and Meditation

That Unknown

I look for the unknown,
I search for it,
I ask questions about it,
But I only hear the silence,
See the dark,
And find a vacuum
Facing me.

I yearn to see it,
I burn to know how it looks,
Wish to take its measures:
Its length and width!
As for its weight,
Well, it,
That enigmatic unknown,
Weighs heavy on me.

This disguised mysterious one,
This wailing, wretched one,
This complaining lucky one,
This contented and satisfied one,
This demented rejecting one,
This enigmatic unknown
Burns my day with anxiety,
Controls my night with insomnia,
Sways my days on a swing,
So they never stay still
It lets them have a taste of bliss,
Intoxicates them with wealth and prestige,
And gives them spring, on a plate,
Then it brings them misery,
Like a slap on the face,
And forces them to partake
Of winter.
They are left no choice,

Can take no decision,
And find themselves being tortured
In the lap of the Inferno.

Undoubtedly you know it,
That which is called
The unknown;
You know it the same way you know
A mirage;
You know it the way you know me,
I, the searcher
For truth,
For a source,
For a destination.
I look among the clouds,
I sink in a labyrinth,
I fall into the heart of mist.
I want to get hold of it;
I want to torment it
The same way I was tormented by it,
That thing which is called the unknown.

O yes, it is
That unknown
Which does not turn up,
Cannot be beaten,
Never retreats,
Nor ever, ever gives up;
It confronts me, fights me, beats me,
And then gets hold of me.
I ask, look, and search,
And I only hear
The echo of silence,
I only see
The reflection of darkness,
And I only touch
A vacuum
That swallows me.

True Love?!

They said about love
That it has a short life
That it dies
In infancy,
Like a blooming flower
Annoyed by butterflies,
Fearful of bees,
And full of loathing for wasps;
Yet, sooner or later,
It bows and yields,
Voluntarily on rare occasions,
Unwillingly in most cases.
That's how love stories are
At all times
And in all places.
They begin with
Shunning,
Annoyance, coyness,
And blushing,
Then comes a temporary triumph,
A passing joy,
And they wither at the end
When a yearning lover
Gets what he has desired and longed for:
A blooming rose
Always has
A short life.

Love lives
A long, long life
Which goes on forever
If it melts,
And then is formed,
By separation and denial.
Love lasts

As long as denial lasts,
And it withers
With intimacy and union.
Love's flame glows and blazes
When intimacy
Is linked to desertion,
When the separation has been long,
And when it is incensed by desertion.
Love, when it is true,
Is an eternal, everlasting spot
In the heart,
Unremovable by casual affairs.
True love
Knows no forgetfulness
And insists on running
Like a wide flowing river
Which waters and irrigates
All the valleys
Of dry lands.

Negative and Positive

Let us imagine life
Without women,
Without the negative, passive part
Which never calms down until
It unites with the positive and active!
Of course we will be relieved
From the chatter,
From nagging,
And exaggerations as well,
And also from never-ceasing
Complaints
And never-abating, never-deterred
Jealousy.
In addition, we will be relieved
From nervous breakdowns,
Childish behaviour,
Sleepless nights,
Song writing,
And attempts to shed tears
Which would wet the cheeks
And seep into
Every single rib.

I have wondered
Millions of times
Would this life on earth
Or the other, immortal life
Be good without her!
Would it be exciting?
Would it be comfortable,
With the negative and passive missing
And the positive and active distracted?
I honestly answered myself,
Repeating with deep earnestness,
That each individual,

Female or male,
Has, in a certain proportion,
Negative and passive signs,
And positive and active ones.
In the beginning
And at the end
We are one individual,
A single integrated person
Who does not settle
Nor calm down
Unless he collides
And then unites.

Music

No to words!
No to expressions!
No to rhyming prose phrases!
No to the ending of verse lines
With rhyming sounds!
Still, I am not judicious,
Nor am I an expert
On dialects and languages.
I am a human being,
Like every other human being
Who has feelings and emotions,
And two ears
Which listen, hear,
And are moved;
Who is either alienated or elated.
If the words are
In his own language,
If the idioms
Belong to his dialect,
And if the tempo
Represents his environment,
He reaches the apex of enjoyment
While he listens.
If he pretends
Otherwise
He is either a good actor
Or a domesticated person
Full of confusion.

When we want to be universal,
To address all humanity,
The language of life,
Of listening elation,
Of exultation and enjoyment,
The language understood by

All human beings,
Is music.
When it is quiet,
And when it is loud and boisterous,
On a solo instrument
Or an instrument ensemble,
Music is man's language
By which he expresses
His joy,
Distress,
Yearning,
Loneliness,
Victory,
Defeat,
True ecstasy,
And false allegiance.

Music is the medium
Human beings use
To influence each other,
To reach into
The depths of the soul,
To provoke sentiments
And move feelings,
To let instincts run wild
Or suppress pain
To stop to exist,
To be reassured
About life and existence,
To express all languages.
For music is
The language understood by
All human beings,
The language of every human being
From the day he arrives
To the day he departs.

The Cat and I!

He asked her,
What's wrong? What happened?
Why is there sadness in your voice?
Has it forgotten its playfulness?
Has it lost its joy?
It is almost toneless,
Without a ring.
Yesterday, she replied,
I greatly suffered;
I stood outside doors
Overcome by
Anxiety and perplexity,
Which surrounded me for a long time.
The reason was a cat
In the street.
She was sitting
Under my balcony
Watching the road
Like a shy child
Fascinated by what she saw
On the road before her eyes.
She was just beautiful.

The cat I was watching,
Like a mother
Watching a child of hers,
Suddenly moved.
She started to cross the road.
All of a sudden she was hit
By metal that was rushing
Along the road.
In a moment I was
At her side; I carried her
And ran with her in my arms
Along the road.

They wouldn't take her
And treat her,
And so, after long suffering, she died.
I was disappointed and frustrated.
I took her back with me
And buried her in my yard
Between flower beds
Under my balcony.

He went into deep thinking.
He told himself,
This is a girl
Whom my mother told me
Not to marry,
Because as my mother saw her
She was quite plain,
In spite of being nice and cheerful.
I respected my mother's wish.
But after what I heard today
I am going to marry her,
Even though I will disobey
My late mother.
I have no reason
Other than being certain
This girl
Will worry about me,
Have pity for me,
And love me
Much more
Than she loved
The cat in the street.

The Virgin?!

Freedom?
What is Freedom?
Who is Freedom?
She is an unmatched beauty.
Whoever gets intimate with her,
Loves her,
And puts her into practice,
Can work miracles with her.
Freedom descended to earth
From the seventh heaven.
Since Adam was cast with Eve
Down to earth,
She has been giving birth
To billions of people
But Freedom has remained
And will always remain
A unique beauty, a virgin,
Since the early dawn of human life
To the last sunset.

Philosophers and thinkers maintain
That everything in this life
Is relative
And that nothing is absolute;
The size of our planet is relative,
Compared to other planets;
My rank is relative,
Compared to other ranks;
Love is relative;
Thirst is relative;
And relative is everything
About life and objects.
I hold the opposite view
And declare
That nothing ever is relative

About Truth or Freedom.
Truth is absolute;
It is God.
And Freedom is an absolute right
For all human beings.

How much has Freedom suffered?
Tyrants and oppressors
Have always been trying
To humiliate her,
Belittle her,
Rob her of her pride,
And molest her maidenhood.
As a result,
Rivers of blood have been shed
All over the world,
For Freedom is a holy virgin.
Whoever insults her will be insulted,
Whoever swears at her will feel sorry,
Whoever damns her will be slain,
And whoever begins with her
Will never reach an end.
It is a weapon given to us
By the Great Giver,
With which to say
To injustice, slavery, and oppression,
And to every argument and excuse,
No, no, no!

God gives us a great example
In upholding and applauding Freedom,
For it was the will of the All-Knowing, Sublime Creator
To create someone who would say
Even to his own Pride, Might, and Grandeur,
No, no, no!
It was Satan, who would not
Prostrate himself to Adam
When all other angels did
At God's order,
And so the Omnipotent, the Merciful
Turned him into Satan the Devil.

Would people then never learn the moral
Of the parables given by the Lord.
No, they have not and will not;
They have fought and will fight
To safeguard and glorify Freedom,
Or to rape and mutilate Freedom,
But Freedom
Will remain a holy virgin
Till Doomsday.

He Made Me Lose Faith in Dreams!

The same way that it happens
To maidens in dreams
While they are asleep,
Or in day dreams
During their waking hours,
The huge, handsome young man,
On his white horse,
Carried me away.
I was unaware
Of what happened
On the first day of the feast.
I thought on that rosy, red night
That the days to come
Would be similar to
That night with its wine-colour.
But fate was quick
And brought in
What I failed to foresee;
The rose, which was me,
Withered and faded
As days passed.

I, the fresh rose,
Was now a companion to grief,
A friend of my sorrows,
Because the knight of my dreams
Was raised with a big ego.
Egoism was his twin brother.
He always takes
And never gives.
He takes what I have,
What is mine,
And wants me (God give me mercy)
To worship him
Rather than God.

He made me lose faith in dreams,
In horses, in feasts,
And in white, blue, red, and pink.
Now I believe in melancholy,
In inferno-like mornings,
Brown afternoons,
Pitch-black nights,
And nightmares of all sorts.
I have dried up.
I am now like a waste desert.
I exist the same way that
Extinction does.

When He Knocked at My Door . . .

Do you know
What winter is?
It is . . . it is the end
Of the smiling, cheerful spring;
The elegant, carefree summer;
And the beautiful autumn,
Donned with the colours of life.
My end was
When he knocked at my door.
I realized it was winter;
I had walked around
In the woods
But could see no trace
Of colour in the trees.
Leaves cracked
As I stepped on them.
I roamed in the wilderness
And heard no nightingale singing.
Brooks were dry
And the wide expanses
Which used to be green
Were now coloured
In pale, timid, resigned,
And mournful yellow.
Seeing this,
I went back to my room.

I went back to my room
And sat on a chair,
Staring at the picture of the walls
Around me,
Recalling events and memories,
Days of the past,
And nights that are gone forever,
My triumphs and defeats,

My mother – oh yes, my mother,
My father, my brother,
My children, my folk,
My mates and my enemies.
Suddenly I saw him
Right in front of me,
His breath blowing on my face,
Finding its way to my bones,
Oozing into my soul,
Penetrating my heart.
My chest and my lungs
Fought to exhale,
Invited and welcomed inhaled air,
Struggled in resistance of
Bitter cold winds
Which enveloped me
On every side.

I did not allow him in;
Winter, like doom, gets in
Without asking for permission,
Through the gap under the door.

We're Getting Close to the End!

Our Author and Creator
Made life of a mixture
Of negative and positive.
In order for life in this world
To grow and go on,
The negative and positive
Must unite.
If two negatives meet
Or two positives unite,
It is a deviation from the order of life,
A violation of life rules,
A significant signal,
A sound and light alarm
Warning us
And drawing our attention,
Telling us in so many words,
That we're getting close to the end,
That we're marching in a great hurry,
On the road of Death,
Towards Doomsday.

A Paradise Made of Plastic

Once I decided
To go out on the street,
Look for a supporter,
Search for a disputer;
I was yearning for a friend;
I greatly value a companion
When I am free from care
And the person I meet
And talk with
Is burdened with a thousand worries.

I mount nothing but my shoes
And am burdened with nothing but thin air.
I walked and walked,
Like cattle on the loose,
Until my way was illuminated
By a bright gleam,
Which guided me into
A grand, wide park
Which seemed green and blooming.
I was at that point
Weary and exhausted,
So I went in, only to discover
That the trees, the grass,
And the flowers
In that park
Were made of plastic.

Once I was inside,
I realized that the owners
Were a clever gang
Of wicked and mean people.
After welcoming me
And fussing over my arrival,
They confiscated and ransacked me.

They placed me in a hall,
Which was rich and big,
And filled with people like me.
They were wicked,
And we were stupid.

On the walls
Pictures appeared in wonderful colours
And on the floor one could see
A banquet of the most delicious food
And sweetest drinks.
After I had calmed down,
They said to me,
'Drink, eat, and watch,
But make sure not to think.
And woe unto you,
If you, having thought,
Move or express yourself.'

In Reality and on Paper

I catch my breath and and think
Of nothing,
For my imagination has dried up
Completely
And when I think,
I meditate nothingness.
Tonight in particular
I am certainly helpless,
Paralyzed,
Not only in reality
But also
On paper.

I have jotted down many lines
On my adventures;
I lied to myself,
To them, and to you;
I claimed as my own deeds
Things that were done by others,
And all this was
On paper.

I put on the garb of religion,
But failed to learn any lesson.
I sprayed sermon
In the air,
And before you I prayed
Both the assigned
And the recommended prayers.
And after arbitrating religious questions,
I ruled that caravans,
Both near and far,
Were bound to get lost.
I hanged dissenters
And burned rejectors

In flaming fire,
And before your eyes,
I went to paradise,
But that was also
On paper.

As for my endless affairs
With love,
My pen was too embarrassed
To tell you
That I had always been the victim,
Always the wronged one,
Often the cheated one.
Even my phrases
Refused to go into the usual routine
And take their usual places
On paper.

I was afraid of writing;
My pen revolted
Against suffering and treachery
And warned me that it would dry up,
Then it was disgusted, it spat,
And stubbornly and insistently
Asked me to try
Another weapon
And to leave and tear up
What I used to write down
Day after day and night after night
On paper.

What do you think?
Things are not clear to me,
And I no longer know.
Do you want me
To give a false image of
Your and my real situation?
Or is it better
To be silent,
To stop
Deceiving myself and you

With my drunk imagination
And my dreams
Which every night I scribble
On paper.

How Can Summer and Winter Meet?

I am cold and inert
Like ice, like winter,
And you are flaming and burning
Like desert summer;
It is my destiny that I should melt
In your summer
And roam in your desert.

How can summer and winter meet
At the same time?
How can snow fall
In summer,
And how can flowers bloom
In winter?
And where is spring?
Where is autumn?
Summer must have
Forgotten spring,
Must have cut it out
And bypassed it,
And winter must have paid
No attention to autumn,
Must have crossed it off
And cancelled it.
Now my years swing
Between the flames of summer
And the ice of winter.

My months only recognize
The fire of summer
And the piles of winter.
My weeks are burning up
With the summer heat
And are trampled
By the feet of winter.

As for my hesitant days
And apprehensive night,
They have reached a decision:
Nights sleep with summer
And days commit suicide
In winter.

I am in a whirlpool of confusion;
My summer is a bullet
And my winter is a gallows.
While spring,
About which I read,
And autumn,
Of which I hear,
Have never paid me a visit.
What am I to do?
I will leave it up
To years, months,
Weeks, nights, and days
To do with me what they will.

The Reign of Frivolity

I did not consult my brain
Nor did I think.
I got myself worked up
And went so far
As to close the doors of my mind.
I tempted my heart
To go to excess on the tracks of love.

My heart soared
In the skies of love,
Then fell down;
It was scorched by denial and separation.
My soul failed to tell me
At the start
That I was being reckless
And foolish,
That I was deriding lovers
And ridiculing the patient,
That I was following
The desert trails of the lost,
That I was one of the missing,
One of the bewildered.

But I did not give in
Nor give up;
I roamed through villages and towns,
Searching for
A magician,
A doctor,
In whom I could confide
And tell the details
Of my case, my suffering
Of my disease.

Every doctor or charlatan

I met
Either was candid with me
Or evaded the truth.
I was frankly told
When my case was deemed
Hopeless,
'Do not consult a doctor;
Seek the advice of
An experienced specialist.'

Should I ask an experienced specialist,
When I am the most experienced
And the best specialist?
I have spent years
Demolishing and erecting,
Calming down to have some rest
Then destroying what I had built,
Hating what I had loved,
And falsifying the truth,
Which chases me to tell me
That my ailment is in my heart
And my medicine is also in my heart,
That I am the victim
Of the reign of frivolity.

The Noose

O my eternal yearning
For your garden!
O my longing, defeated
By the heat of your rejection!
O my passion, confused
Between your satisfaction and displeasure!
One time I chant and sing
In your heaven,
Another time I suffer
In your hell,
And a third I am the hanged man,
Swinging between the two.

They say you must
Stand in the middle,
And yet you have seen
What happened to me in the middle!
Excuse and forgive me;
My experience pushed me
To go to the extreme,
Allowed me no room
To maneuver:
Either bliss in her heaven
Or doom in her hell.

You wonder and feel astonished
At my situation and my condition!
Do not wonder,
No, nor be astonished!
I was myself that way
When I was shallow,
Having explored no depth
At all;
I was simple and naive,
Having not been introduced

To waves yet,
Not taken a ride on them,
Nor understood their meaning
When they approach
Or their significance
As they retreat.
I was the laughing stock of lovers!

And so
My yearning will last;
It will not be defeated
By your hell.
My longing will continue
In spite of your rejection.
And my passion will persist and persist
Whether you are satisfied
Or displeased!
As for you,
Your fire will subside and die out,
Your heaven will be consumed
By drought,
And as for me,
The years have taught me
How to evade the noose!

PART FIVE

Bewildered Sighs

Would I Find a Medicine?

When my tears had dried,
Bewilderment had overtaken my soul,
And my face had been frowning,
I received an order
From my inner self
That I should be able
To distinguish,
Should be determined
To focus,
Should get free
From painful memories;
That my thoughts should resign
And stop colonizing my heart;
That I should give
A grand, lavish party
To my defeats and my triumphs.

I gave a grand, lavish,
Boisterous party
And invited the mutilated
And confused images of the past.
I made a drink
Out of the cool breeze
And cooked a dish
Of sprinkling ashes.
I hid among the strings
Of players.
The singer sang
A cold number
With a cold tune
Played on static instruments,
Which neither communicated
Nor responded,
So the notes died
Of chill.

In my following days
I rode my towering waves
And sailed the seas of love.
My heart went up and fell.
It went up,
But failed to reach the moon,
And fell,
But reached no bottom.
It got lost in passion
Among the waves of bewilderment.

How I regret what has gone,
How sorry I am for my present,
And how fearful of what is to come.
Is it my doom to be never away
From tears?
Is it my destiny not to have my heart
Between my ribs,
To have it roam
On the pavements of frustration,
To have my shoulders
Overburdened with worries?
And when I find
A clearing among the clouds
Of melancholy
And want to think of my future,
Is it my fate to be faced
With exclamation points
And question marks?

How can my soul be washed
And cleansed of what is past?
How can I cure the wounds
Of emotion and love?
Will my pains continue to ooze
For ever?
Will I remain a slave
Of imaginings and digression?
And who would lend me a vessel
That would carry and endure me?
Now, let me suppose my desire

Is granted
And I did find supplies
And a vehicle,
Would I find a medicine?

I Find Shelter in Silence

Loneliness used to torment me.
Estrangement used to kill me.
When I dreamt, while being alone
With objects,
I would jump from sleep
As if I had
A burning nightmare.

A cat, any cat,
Kept me company;
An insect, any insect,
Made me laugh;
Companionship, in any form,
Gave me pleasure;
A woman, whoever she was,
Made me happy;
I used my friend
For support;
And seeing my enemy
Made me ready and anxious
For war.

Estrangement always was
The source of my distress;
It was the blade
Which aimed to kill me,
As if I were a fruitful palm tree
Uprooted from an oasis
Of Arabia,
Full of palm trees,
And carried in an airplane,
And the tall and dark trunk
Was planted
Into a deep valley in the North
That never has warmth,

Or like a bedouin
Who was seized with all his property,
Then was left alone
To search for pasture
In the wilderness of frost.

In my dreams, while I slept,
Looking at objects
Terrified me;
I found comfort in living along
With all other living creatures:
A wolf would play with me,
A snake would dance with me,
And a scorpion's poison never killed me;
And I overflowed with hope
And ambition
When I was with a human being.

But now I have lost
My trust in man,
My love for animals is dead,
And I have kicked out of my room
The insects I got intimate with.
Now . . . now
Tall trees do not fascinate me,
And blooming flowers,
Fragrant roses,
Life and the living
Mean nothing to me.
I found shelter
In silence.

Why is it, why?
Why am I like this?
Because man in this age
Is deformed and treacherous,
Mothers' milk
Is powdered and canned,
A rooster is a lord,
Chicken eggs
Are produced in factories

And hatched by machines,
Fruits are orphans
Snatched away from their mothers,
Flowers are sterile,
Roses are dreary
Like figures
In wax museums,
Horses are mongrels;
Fish are half-breed,
Wheat stalks have been persuaded
To grow and multiply
In stagnant water,
And even the aunt of all,
The palm tree,
Has been fooled and is now watered
By illegitimate money.

And now . . . now
That my brain is like
Inanimate objects,
That my minutes have been ground,
Like dust,
That my hours turned
Into rocks,
And that my day and night
Are like mountains –
Now, now
I do not see, nor hear, nor feel,
And I find shelter
In silence.

This Is My Tragedy

In my imagination and in reality,
Letters jump and scatter around;
I have no desire to collect them,
I wish them to disperse,
I determine to keep them away,
I do not want them to get intimate
Or to unite,
So that no word would be born.
Yet, in spite of me,
Each letter takes its right position,
And its proper ring in the ear,
And I am tormented
By the multiplication of words.
Then I suffer
A new demand;
Words want to be connected.
I reprimand and rebuke them,
But against my will,
They proliferate and form,
Making a sentence.
Still the letters are not content;
One sentence does not satisfy them.
So, out of several sentences,
Paragraphs pour like rain.
This is my tragedy.

The same way that each of us
Has wishes and ambitions,
Sentences are like human beings;
Unless they express something,
They die and cease to be.
Therefore, they are not
Satisifed and content
By the torment I have with letters
Nor by my suffering with words;

They are rather determined
To express honestly
My most inner depths;
They want me to write them down,
To document them
On paper
And sign my name under them.
They want my recognition.
No ... no ... no!
Let letters curse me!
No ... no ... no!
Let words slap me!
No ... no ... no!
Let sentences wound me!
No ... no ... no!
Let paragraphs hang me!
Never ... never ... never
Will I recognize them,
And I will take refuge
In the castles of silence.

Days

I work hard and toil.
I make happy days,
Which I try to get
To pile and multiply.
I manage to fly with them
Far, far away
From bewilderment and jealousy,
From misery and despair,
From tempters and evil-whisperers,
Whether jinn or human beings.
I bury them deep,
Like a careful experienced person
Who knows his way.

When I need them,
I search for them;
I look in my store;
I rummage with my hands;
I search in my mind,
In my memory,
In my soul,
In my heart;
And I scrutinize with my eyes
For the happy days
Which I worked hard to make,
But I only find
Some soft sand
Which managed to pass through my sieve
And was hit, dispersed,
And scattered
In the deserts of bewilderment
By hostile winds.

I look at my sieve
And only see holes,

Each is like an eye
Abused by time,
So it cannot wink, close,
Or sleep.
They seem to say to me,
'Look for happiness,
For pleasure and merriment,
For the fire of love,
In a clogged sieve,
Which must be enchanted
And sealed by Satans.'

But I know that a sieve
With tight joints
And plugged holes,
Is like a sheet of iron
Or an obtuse asphalte road;
Things get mixed on it;
It does not feel thirsty,
Nor does it drink;
It is neither watered,
Nor does it quench the thirst.
It has lukewarm feelings;
It does not get disgusted,
Nor does it laugh,
And it makes no distinction
Between gems and garbage.

I Want to Die Standing

I am going to die.
Yes, I will perish!
Yes, I will come to an end!
This is an old-new truth
Which I try to ignore.
But how am I going to die?
Only He, the All-Knowing, knows.
But I wish,
I beseech the All-Knowing
To let me die standing
Like ancient trees,
Which are erect when they die;
They die standing.
I would hate to die
In my bed,
Surrounded by others
Who would wait for my departure,
While I am in a conflict
Between my survival instinct
And the inevitability of death.

Prisoner of a Mirage?!

My ship went too far
On the Sea of Ambition.
It had not a single calm day.
Not once did it get to know
A clean port.
Waves carried it high
To a climax
And brought it down
To the lowest level,
And between the climax and the lowest level,
It was always
In the heart of mist
Struggling with the unknown,
Ever, always,
Contesting and maneuvering,
Gaining and losing ground,
But it never got away
From the surging and colliding waves,
Nor out of the mist cavity.
Today my ship is
Broken and helpless,
Having been lost in the mist,
And made by the torrent
A prisoner of a pirate
Named Mirage.

Especially You, Enemies

Suddenly, while I was at the climax
Of joy and happiness,
Time, without any warning,
Dealt me two blows.
I bore the first;
Savage as it was, I absorbed it.
As for the second, oh how bad it was!
How terribly it made me suffer!
I am fed up of talking about it,
I beg you to be patient,
And I ask you to forgive me:
I have suffered a lot
To be able to write these words,
The introduction of which
Is already too long.
For, dear readers,
I feel certain that you
Have not yet heard my story,
Because I am weary
Of all the things I have been telling
About the drowning of my joy
And the suicide of my delight.
I am determined that you should know –
Oh, sorry, I have changed my mind;
You are not going to know,
Especially you, enemies!

Desperate Hope

During my calm,
Which is charged with anger,
During my upright,
Furious anxiety,
On the bed of sleeplessness,
When my soul is lost
In the routes of ashes
Or in the flames of fire,
My achievements fade,
My triumphs are routed,
And I can only discern and see
My desperate ambitions
And a facsimile
Of a wreck that used to serve
As a fortress for my thoughts.
I insist on looking
In heaps of dirt,
And I resolve to dive
In stagnant swamps,
Searching for remains,
For the wreckage,
For the old,
For the new,
For what I have fought
To bring out,
And for what I have suffered
In order to hide.

My brain is like a sickle,
Cutting and making no distinction
Between green and dry;
My memory is like a sieve
Through which
My happiness and joys pass,
Leaving nothing on it

But hard rocks
That pose as enemies.
I try to fling them away;
I make an effort to bury them
In the heart of nothingness,
But they resist me,
Turn back towards me,
Aim at me and hit me,
And I drown and linger
In a sea of pain.

O my renewed hope
That toys with me!
O my paralyzed love
That frustrates me!

My hope,
My love,
Where are you both?
You, my hope,
Deceive me.
You are my devil,
My volcano,
That covers with lava
My valleys and my shores,
Tortures my trees,
Kills my birds,
Exhausts my supplies,
Threatens my sea and lakes
With bitter taste and dryness,
And turns my land
Into a flat rock,
A barren, cold, and dull rock,
So my love can find
No warm womb,
And it gets paralyzed and then dies
Before it can hear
My voice.

I Have Decided Not to Sleep

When I sleep I am attacked
By nightmares,
I found myself bound
In chains,
Surrounded by walls,
Watched by spies.
Screams of horror envelop me;
I tremble and gasp
And I wake up from reality,
Upright like a pillar,
Wet out of fear,
Terrified at what I have seen,
Aching because of what I have suffered,
My heart beats
Faster than my breath.
I get tired, I collapse,
And I go back to sleep,
But nightmares come back to me,
Capture me!
From my experience with sleep,
With the torture of nightmares
And anxiety,
I have learned that my salvation
Can only be by being awake,
So I decided not to sleep.
I will never, ever sleep.

It Was My Heart That Cried

Who was it that made my grief?
Who was it that awakened my regret?
Was it my disappointment?
Was it the triumph of my fear
Over my courage and daring?
Or did destiny,
Out of nothingness,
Bestow foliage
On the branches of grief and regret
Stemming from the trunk of my misery?

I ask my own entity
And address the question to you:
Are grief and regret the outcome
Of an illicit affair
Between bafflement and jealousy,
Or between calm and madness?
My entity does not exactly know
The reason of my grief and regret.
It was my soul that took the decision,
While my mind was neutral,
And my heart cried
In broad daylight.
It paid no attention
To the rituals of grief
Or the protocol of regret
Which both dictate that crying
Should be in neglected shadows
Or in forgotten basements.
I accuse myself
Of treason and intrigue
And I am indicted by my brain
With cowardice and feebleness.

The question is still posed

And valid,
And my entity has lost hope;
It is unable
To answer that question.
War rages between
My imaginings, my thoughts,
And my feelings.
My emotions never surrender;
They resist with stubbornness and determination,
But, alas,
They lose the battle.

Who was it that made my grief?
Who was it that awakened my regret?
Give me an honest answer,
A brief answer!
Was it
My own self?
Or did you all
Plot together?
Answer me! Answer me!
Who has posed the question?
Who knows the answer?!
?!
O how baffled I am!

I Don't Know, I Cannot Tell

My joys and my smiles
Raced to greet you
At your arrival.
My joy did not win,
Nor did my smiles lose:
They arrived together
At the time of your arrival.

My heart gave
An exquisite wedding party,
Invited my organs and my senses,
And offered my yearning as a drink
And my love as food.
As for lovers' words
The language of loving reproof,
And the expressions of joy –
They were the opening
Of the wedding ceremony
In which the bride and bridegroom
Were happiness and your presence.

Your arrival was like light
That stirs a breeze,
Works it up, makes it blow
On a flower bed,
So that the fragrance of perfume
Would accompany your steps.
The way your hair moves
Is like a storm,
Like wild wind,
Which roars and rages,
And swirls and surges
To tell those who are present
That it is here,
Here with me,

To demolish and eliminate
My unhappiness.

Do I live in reality?
Or am I a simpleton,
Feeding on chronic delusion;
Setting objects,
People, and creatures
To all run
After a fantasy which is hooked
On day dreams;
And insistently weaves a tent
To set up
On a sea surface?
I don't know what is going on!
I don't know, I cannot tell!
Do you understand what I mean,
What I have written and am saying?

PART SIX

I? Who Am I?

I? Who Am I?

They say
That I am a great actor,
That had Sir Laurence Olivier
Seen me
He would have certainly been jealous.
As for you, if you see me
You will say that
I am a true master of my art,
And that I certainly know
How to hide my true identity.
With the manager, for instance,
I learned,
As soon as I was employed,
Two important words,
'OK' and 'yes,'
And with all my superiors,
I use with 'yes,'
All expressions of esteem and respect,
And all exaggerated terms of exaltation.
When I want to leave,
I walk backwards,
With my tongue wetting my lips
With a smile full of hope.
And I bow
So that my upper half
Makes a right angle
With my lower one.

I insist, and I challenge
Anyone to prove the opposite,
That if I have opponents
Or enemies,
I treat them with equal
Amounts of flattery and hypocrisy.
No one really knows me

And my natural behaviour,
Except the members of my family.
I hardly ever allow my servant,
The servant of my sons and daughters,
To have medical treatment or medicine;
I only give her
Old, worn-out clothes
And what food we loath.
In the room of my sons
I have planted a tree,
The branches of which
Are the letters of 'no,'
And the leaves are
'Forbidden' and 'not allowed.'
As for my daughters' room,
I have decorated it,
With the words 'denied' and 'banned.'
And when I think of my wife,
I sigh –
Having given up all hope
That I might change
And modify my conduct,
She had a heart attack
And passed away.

Am I a Beast or a Human Being

In my contradictory evenings,
During the conflicting hours of my night,
I rage like a bull,
Calm down like a dove,
Laugh like a moron,
Mock with malice,
Roar with deep guffaws,
Play tricks,
And amuse myself with fooling
Simple folks.

In my diminishing evenings,
During the last hours of my night,
I am delighted by remote memories
And have no tolerance for
My recent follies.
I blame myself
For what I have done,
And rebuke myself
For what I have failed to do.
I get lost in persistent loss.
I sit with periods,
Sleep upon time,
And wake up feeling afraid
Of being lost.

In my erect evenings,
During the darting hours of my night,
I fight against the prevailing black
To win the bright white,
So that no black colour would invade
A rising dawn.
But the black
Tempts to indulge myself
And darkness makes me forget,

Induces me to
An incomplete war,
And drags me into
A dying battle
In which I can only win
A mirage.

In my ripe evenings,
During the surging hours of my night
I am enchanted
With the language of a lute,
Intoxicated
By the goblets of a violin,
And moved by the beat of tambourines.
I drown in a distressed tune
Which hungrily banters
With my sorrows.
It goes too far
And clothes my miseries
In a gown of tears,
Leaving me a prisoner
Of distraction.

In my angry evenings,
During the averse hours of my night,
My thoughts clamour
With exhaustion,
My pen overflows
With reproof,
Letters burn my paper,
My rage makes the words drop down,
And my malice wipes out the books.

O my angry, ripe, erect,
Contradictory,
Diminishing evenings;
O averse, surging,
Darting, lost,
Conflicting hours
Of my night –

Am I a beast
Or a human being?

I Am a Different Beast!

At the peak of my anger,
At the climax of my joy,
I am a different beast,
I mean I am
A different person,
An abnormal, discordant human being,
Which is the reason of my unhappiness.
All people, or rather
Most people,
Show something different from
What they feel inside.
With me, it is the other way around.
At the climax of my joy,
I recall the stabs;
I announce to all
The wrongs that have been done to me,
While at the peak of my anger,
Happiness is available at hand;
It watches and witnesses
The explosion of my wrath
And cries with many tears.
My sordid moments of love
Also flee
From between my ribs.
I am not sure
Whether you agree
With my conviction
That I am abnormal and discordant.

No Doubt I Am the Madman!

You provoke my jealousy,
You set my madness free,
Out of its prison,
With the whispers and intimacy
You have with my foe and rival
And hide from me.
If my misgivings and suspicions
Get the better of me,
If I am destroyed by my jealousy
And makes friends with my madness,
Beware!

You say you're free?
What about me?
It was you who possessed me
After you had crowned me
With the crown of love.
Now you betray me,
Sell at a very cheap price
Our rivers of honey,
And buy at outrageous prices
Imitation jewelry.

From now on,
Colocynth will be sweet to me,
Masquerades and I will have a laugh,
And I will dance with a mirage,
Chat with anxiety,
Stay up late with misgivings,
Shut out happiness and joy,
Make jokes
At myself,
But will not
Allow you to get hold of me
Ever again.

Do you know what suffering is?
Do you know what bitter reproof means?
Do you know what punishment
You deserve?
Don't you know that the evening
Mocks daylight?
Don't you know that darkness
Grinds the evening
Every night
In order for a new dawn
To rise every day?
And so it is with love,
Hatred, and lies.
So it is with freedom,
Slavery, and domination.

What shall I tell you?
That you have aborted my dreams
And confused my words?
That my lines were astonished
At the flaming heat of my sentences
And my papers ran away
From my pens?
I am not unsettled,
Most confused;
Who am I?

I started with poetry,
With most elegant rhymes.
I went back to ancient poems
And glorified sorrow and ruins.
I ended with words
As loud as cannon balls,
Demolishing with their shells
My steel prison house,
Which was fortified
With the impossible;
My desperate grief,
Which was trained to be sad;
And my miserable yearning,
Which got accustomed to pain.

I scribble in a hurry
Some lines
Which I am forced
To erase in a hurry.
I disassemble my words,
Cast my letters
In the waste basket of madness.
I? Who am I?
No doubt I am the madman.

We, the Artist, Sanctify Freedom

I adore the brush
As it flirts with landscapes
On canvas
Or on paper,
Using familiar, traditional,
Serene colours
Or an outrageous,
Bold, conflicting mixture,
Which breaks away with tradition
And allows the artist to create
An extraordinary dialogue
Between the brush and colours,
And between nature and man.
It rouses the consciousness
And stimulates the senses,
So the viewer is astonished
Or finds comfort
In the calm and serenity,
Or the rebellion and madness,
On a piece of canvas or of paper.

I am infatuated by fingers
Which touch with their tips
Any musical instrument
And, with determination, express
My tense anxiety,
My continuous sleeplessness,
My obvious jealousy,
My fervent love,
My wavering hope,
And my burning ambition
To reach
The climax of perfection.

I am the poet

Who gets hold of words,
Tames and trains them,
Teaches them good manners,
Gets them to think,
Makes them express,
And forms them into
Necklaces of jewelry
That can be made
Only by angels.
I am the poet
Who chisels out of languages
Monuments and statues
Which, like living creatures,
Storm out in a tremendous demonstration,
Waving red flags
With the colour of blood,
Roaring like cannons,
Warning like thunderstorms,
Throbbing with humanity,
Shining with pride,
Gleaming with dignity,
Flying with freedom,
And cursing humiliation and slavery
Throughout their immortal life.

We are the artist,
Who gives to life
A rhyme and a reason
With music, with colours,
With numbers, with words,
And with voice volumes;
Who expresses and interprets,
In short or in detail,
Love, hope,
Separation, pain,
Birds, the sea,
Angels, human beings,
Cursed devils,
And the charitable righteous;
Who kisses rain,
Mud, and soil;

Who pines away for love, anxiety,
Jealousy, or sleeplessness;
And who makes no distinction
Between facts and illusions,
Or between reality and the imagination.
We, the artist,
Let go;
We fear no danger,
Refuse humiliation,
Sanctify freedom,
And worship God.

You, I, and Time!

How seconds make
Me suffer;
How they, like wishes, slowly crawl.
How lazy and inactive they are!
How like turtles!
They walk in place,
Retreat forward,
As if they were a mosque speaker
Delivering his Friday speech,
Always repeating
The same worn-out points,
The exact outmoded expressions.

How heavy minutes are!
How similar to tons of data!
Heavy, heavy, heavy!
Grinding my dreams,
Crushing my imaginings,
Striving to cut
Through my waiting location,
Which is fortified with difficulties,
An easy, open route,
Which would lead me to fly
From the gallows of sins
And take me to safety.

No, no, never!
I will not tolerate the rancour of hours;
Their bitter taste runs
In the veins of my being
And all the arteries of my eloquence.
It slaps my times,
Wounds and forces them,
Compels and oppresses them.
It destroys the tender walls of my heart

And replaces them with
Barbed wire,
Which pulls down my love and friendship,
And spills the blood of my joys
Thousands and thousands of times.

My days ride
On top of me,
And on the bottom,
They shake and make me shake;
They never settle
In any form.
The shaking takes my days
For a moment,
But only a moment,
To banquets of joy,
But they remain vigilant and alert.
They do not fail to drag me;
On purpose, they pushed me
In moments
To the valleys of privation,
And my days are buried
In the ingratitude of mates
And in the lairs of toil.

My weeks curse me;
Hungry, they scream
Right in my face.
They ask for something to be said,
They beg for bread,
They implore me for words
That would keep them upright,
Urge them to stand erect,
Keep them from relaxing,
Warn them against falling.
I stand listening
To what I do not comprehend,
And my weeks have
A nervous breakdown.

Meanwhile my months

Are angry at me
And have deserted me
For young and active months,
Past months
Which swarmed with fancies
And teemed with dreams,
And in which reality dried up,
So they ran to the impossible.
They are always this way:
Yearning, sighing, getting mad,
Laughing like imbeciles
And, like human beings,
Desiring what is forbidden
And indifferent to danger.

Years pile on my chest,
One year on top of another,
On top of another,
Glued with a material that reacted
With a tiny bit of the substance
Of happiness
And a great amount
Of the substances of misery.
All pile on my chest,
On layer on top of another,
On top of another.
They keep me from breathing
And kill me
Once
And for all.

PART SEVEN

You and I Are Adam and Eve!

You and Me

When I am with you I feel
That I am a child or a teenager.
I feel in your look
My mother's tenderness
And in your words
My sister's responsiveness,
Yet still
You pose
Difficult questions
In a language
I cannot decipher
In spite of your repetitions.

You say, for instance,
That it is common for people
To get married in holiday seasons,
Although we have never
Discussed the question of marriage;
I am younger than you,
You would not accept me
As a husband,
And I depend on you:
You are discreet,
And I am a reckless adolescent;
You're intelligent and mature
And I am indolent, like snow,
Like all my mates,
Or rather like some of my mates.

My father is dead, and my mother is at a loss
Between my sister, the neighbor,
And her work in the morning.
In you I find
The mother I am missing
And my sister who is busy

With her engagement and
The arrangements for her marriage.
In you I find
My father who taught and advised me.
And now you tell me
You're getting engaged.

Tell me the truth;
Who is proposing to you?
Who is going to snatch you?
I only want
To make sure that I
Won't be lonely
Once you are married:
Today you are my sister;
Tomorrow you will be
My father and mother;
And I won't be able to find
My way in this life without you.

You really want to know?
Hasn't it crossed your mind
All through our long acquaintance
That I like you
And you like me,
That with you I satisfy
My motherhood instinct,
And with me
You merge into life;
That it is you who will propose to me;
That you are my beloved;
And that we will get married
One night
Of the holiday seasons?

You and My Imagination

You lie when you say
You do not know
That I love you?
Don't you believe that?
Ask my heart!
You do not answer.
What are you saying?
Oh, all hearts have chimes,
All hearts make sighs,
All hearts play
The same sad tune
And are frustrated by sober rejection.

Don't you believe that?
Ask this rose!
What I told her
To say.
No, ask that star
What she did when she found out
That I love you?
No, no, no,
Ask your hair,
Ask your cheeks and lips,
Ask your chest,
Ask your eyes and ears
What they see
And what they hear?
Faked love talk,
Deceptive hope,
Or true devotion
And true signs of love?
You do not answer.
What are you saying?
Oh, you're thinking and pondering.

Don't you believe that?
Ask your perfume,
Ask your boudoir,
Ask every atom in your body
About my imagination,
How it was intoxicated
With your perfume,
How it sneaked
Into your boudoir
When you were most beautiful,
How it tore all covers
And your night gown
And seized, without hesitation,
Your heart
And your most private secrets,
How, how, and how?
Ask how it awakened
From the daydream,
Was crushed by despair
Into flour
To make bread
Which all lovers
Are forced
To eat!

Adam and Eve 1

I am a father of six girls.
The first is my experiment field,
Most of my ambitions,
All my presumptions,
My aspiration and my hope.

The second remains my Achilles' heel:
If she gets angry I cannot sleep,
Nor can I sleep when she laughs.
To please her is my concern.

The third remains my pet:
She gets from me whatever she wants
Whenever she wants it.
If she smiles, my happiness has no limit,
And if she cries, my tears are faster than hers.

The fourth is my lyric,
All my poems;
Her joy is the world's joy;
Her grief is grief for the whole globe;
If she is scared or frightened,
My power surges
And my courage mounts,
And I fight the whole world for her sake.

The fifth is my exact image,
And as it is with my mother,
I never think of making her angry.
No, I'll never make her angry.
She orders and I obey; she asks and I comply.
She captures me with her abundant joy.
Deprives me of my will,
Manipulates me as she wishes.
I love her, I love her, I love her.

And I won't find the right words to glorify her name.

The sixth is the last of the lot,
The prettiest girl;
Her eyes teach me what delight is;
Her smile is my heaven;
Her displeasure is my hell.
She is sweeter than honey.

My daughters, my love, my whole happiness,
I and you are
Adam and Eve.

Adam and Eve 2

Eve, full of hope and joy,
Tells her astonished friends,
'Had he not flown thousands of miles
For my sake;
Abandoned the foreign land
And the foreign lady
For my sake;
Returned to settle down,
As he had been,
Near me;
Asked about me,
In the morning and in the evening,
His sister, his cousin,
His mother, and his aunts –
Hadn't he once again attracted me,
Once again proposed to me,
Once again cried
On my chest,
Begged and implored me,
Invoked my love and devotion
To God and God's messenger
To get me to accept him once again –
Hadn't Adam been my beloved,
Done all that I have mentioned,
And said all that I haven't mentioned
Of sweet talk,
Love expressions,
And poems of yearning –
I wouldn't have returned to him;
Eve wouldn't have returned
To Adam!'

Adam and Eve 3

You approach!
Listless and oblivious you approach;
Merry and laughing you approach;
Or frowning and angry you approach,
And still I am the same,
You find me the same as I used to be
And as I still am:
My arms are spread out with craving,
Open and stretched with eagerness,
To meet and embrace you,
For of all places
You can only settle down
And only find comfort
In them.
On my chest
You calm down, settle, and sleep;
Under my wing,
You play, have fun, and sing;
In my face
You rage and get mad;
But your home is always in my arms.
You come back to my ribs
Where you were created,
As Eve was and still is
A rib in Adam's chest,
Next to his heart.

Adam and Eve 5

You get lost in the valley of anxiety,
And hold to the rope of mirage.
You are crushed by the machines of sleeplessness
Due to jealousy, misgivings, suspicions,
And all the causes of madness;
You talk to the curtains,
Hit the pillow,
Quarrel with the bed cover,
And then sit on the bed,
Licking your tears
And starting the argument
All over again
Between your mute brain
And your evil-inclined soul.
Your aim is to raid Adam,
Get hold of him and his domain
By any means
And in every way.
You spring up, thinking and wondering
In the vacuum of the night.
You turn on the lights in your room
To overcome your loneliness
And run to look for a mirror
To look at your face.
You spend hours
Watching your figure,
And spend so much time
Pinching your cheeks,
Biting your lips,
Combing your hair,
And trying various smiles
And all kinds of laughs.
Then you put on a scented nightshirt,
Take a sleeping pill,

Fall into sound sleep,
And dream of Adam.

Adam and Eve 7

You have contrived a plot
And used
Some most recent inventions
To catch me,
Drag me to your trap
And imprison me in your stronghold.

No, no, you have to be a witch,
Or else how come I know when you are away
That you're worried and awake,
Or calm and asleep;
That you remember me
Or are too busy with other things?
How come I know while you're remote
That you haven't read my letters,
Nor worn over your chest
My talismans and charms;
That my picture is folded;
That my gift is not opened,
Just like my scattered papers
And my neglected, forgotten
Sighs and yearnings.

What do you mean?
What do you want?
I have forgotten to remember,
It didn't occur to me to think,
How it was possible for me
To note in the cells of my heart and brain
All this and other things.
Well, now I get it;
You must have planted in my chest
A receiving station;
You must have hooked it
To my veins

To make it run through my whole being,
So that I may receive
Your movements and your tranquil moments.
In my belief, this certainly is
A careful plot
Concocted by Eve
Against Adam.

Adam and Eve 9

Love asked me,
'What are you going to do with her?'
'She is a female,' I said,
'And I am a man.
I will hide the white of my beard
With dyes
And the snow on my head
Also with dyes.
I will restore to my aspect
Its youthfulness and brightness
And to my lyrics
Their themes of love and infatuation,
For maidens are well pleased
With compliments and flattery,
Which are the arms I use with them.'

Love said, 'But she's too young.
Had you been married
She would be at least the same age
As your daughter
And perhaps your granddaughter.
How do you want her for your wife?'
I said, 'How come that you, love,
Inspirer of my poetry,
Source of my rivers,
My master and subduer,
My monarch and sovereign,
Taunt me as if I were
Over ninety,
When it is you yourself, love,
That has abolished all distinctions
In love,
And built for love a kingdom
With a constitution which states
That the relationship between lovers,

Between Adam and Eve,
Is not dependent on years.'

Adam and Eve 11

My poems make you jealous;
You stay up all night
Trying to decipher
The codes of one
Of my clauses
Or to interpret one
Of my words.

You are foolish,
Reckless,
And naive;
You think I write love lines
To someone else, a rival of yours,
Although you well know
That for me you have no competitor
And no rival.
But you are a female,
And like every other female,
You always try
To create for yourself a rival
Who envies you, quarrels with you,
Hates you, and feels malice towards you,
Even when the whole thing
Is a figment of the imagination.

I swear to you, believe me!
Oh, no, you won't believe
That I love you,
I adore you,
And you are my only concern;
You are the pillow
Which brings rest and sleep
To my eyes;
You are the phantom
That scalds me with lack of sleep;

You are coolness in summer,
Warmth in winter,
My song in spring,
And my sadness in autumn;
And I and you are,
At the beginning and in the end,
Adam and Eve.

Adam and Eve 13

Love on my pillow,
Passion on your bed,
Is calm like an ancient volcano,
Tranquil like a lighthouse
Looking over a raging sea.
It gets restless with a mysterious fear,
And humbly recognizes
An alert,
Sick and loathsome villain.
It refuses to utter
A truthful word
Out of perplexed fear,
A lasting fear,
Which pours tragedy into the heart,
Drags it on a hollow route,
Seals it inside a magic bottle,
And casts away in a waste desert.
. . .
You and I are
Adam and Eve.

Adam and Eve 14

Your eyes are a wide and
Mysterious lake,
Capable of getting hold
Of the sea
And of making it
Change the course of its life,
Changing its flow
Into ebb.

And your hair?
Your let-down hair
Or your scattered hair,
Your loose hair
Or your tied-up hair,
Like a soft shore, inhabited
With musk, perfume, and incense,
Leads me on
To an enchanted cave,
Where on the ceilings are inscribed,
And on the walls are written,
The legends of the great love
Anter had for Abla,
Qais for Laila,
Jamil for Buthaina,
Katheer for Azza,[1]
And Romeo for Juliet.

And your smile?
What about your smile?
Your smile calls me,
Proudly implores,
Richly begs,

---

[1] All these are famous lovers in Arabic lore. The first name in each line is for the male lover.

That I should swim
In the sea of love
And be one of the sides
Of the conflict,
Or that I should be a target
For the arrows flying
Out of the perfection of beauty
And the splendour of loveliness.

My fantasies darkened
While I felt for your doors.
My keys are lost;
Your doors will not open.
I have discovered that I
Placed my fantasies, my dreams,
My madness, and my illusions
In your warehouse.
After forgetting,
I now remember
That fantasy and dreams
Are our bread and drink,
That if I eat
You get full
And if I drink
Your thirst is quenched,
And that I am Adam
And you are Eve.

Adam and Eve 17

I remembered and missed you
While storming, roaring winds
Toyed with me and the plane
The same way that in days of the past
Winds toyed with our love,
For storms rerun
Upon the memory screen
Dark pictures.
Fleeting lightnings reveal,
And their bright light illuminates,
Pictures of the crisis
With the same characters and props
Which almost uprooted
Our love,
Almost hurled it away,
Crushed it, scattered it
In all directions,
And planted suspicion
In our confused hearts,
Sowing them in the land of drought
And irrigating them from the river of bitterness.

I drowned in a sea
Of immobile, sleeping tears,
And still they neither woke up
Nor fell;
They rather slept
In memory valleys
And froze
In the sea of escape.
I paid attention only
As the plane
Was landing in safety,
The same way it was with our love
When it bowed

To the storm.
. . .
. . .
I and you are
Adam and Eve.

Adam and Eve 18

I now loathe ornaments;
I have been breaking my jewelry,
Have abandoned my elegance,
As well as parties and visits,
Since I have known
That you wanted me
A wife and a companion
Of whose noble descent you can boast
And who can dazzle with her beauty
The dwellers of mansions.
I have been assured
That my parents and folks
Are leaving the matter up to me,
That if I wished I could accept you
And if I wished I could reject you,
And I am really relieved.

It is true you are a tycoon,
One of the few great tycoons of your generation,
But I am one of the few
Who are in the know;
It has been whispered to me
By those who are experts
In matters of family lineage
That you are of a humble descent;
You are not like my father.
You are also an unnatural person,
A crooked man
Who has no moral values
And no faith
And has a lot and lot of money.

Do you think, or rather imagine,
That your coffers, mansions,
Airplanes, yachts,

Appearance, and youth
Would make me accept you.
No, my noble descent has taught me
That you, and those like you,
Want a flower
To decorate your vase.
You wouldn't care for my heart or brain,
For my conscience and my radiance.
You would merely expect
That my body and soul
Would respond
To everything you would wish.

You want to possess a tame cat
Of a good pedigree
Or an expensive piece of furniture
To entertain yourself with or to move
From one hall in your mansions
To another
In order to be seen and admired
By your guests and visitors.
Or perhaps you need
An exquisite pen
To write with
And then use to sign
Your dubious deals.

Quite simply,
And in spite of any consequent complications,
I reject you, reject you, reject you!
. . .
. . .
You and I are
Adam and Eve.

She: No and Yes

When I was a teenager
And waited on my father's guests,
I always paid attention
To one of his friends.
There was nothing particular about the man,
Nor did he look impressive,
But he spoke wisdom
Concerning the other sex,
Concerning women,
For according to him,
He married twenty-three times.
He often frightened me
And rarely pleased me
With the stories he told
About women
And how to deal
With women.
At that age,
I imagined women to be
Like angels, like my mother.
Yet I will never forget
One wise thing he said
About women
Which may be summed up as
'No' and 'Yes.'

My father's old friend
Used to say,
'Never say to a female,
"All right," or "Yes,"
But always say, "No,"
Even before you understand
What she is asking
Or asking for.
You make her mad

If you say, "Yes,"
Then hesitate
And say, "No,"
And you make her happy
With a definite "Yes"
After an absolute "No."
A woman adores a bridle
When it is
In a man's hand
And scorns a man
Who fails to hold
The leash tight,
Allows a halter
To be loose,
And always says to her,
"All right," and "Yes." '

One of the wise things
The old man, my father's friend,
Said about women,
About woman nature
And instincts,
Is that a woman asks
And keep asking and asking;
If you give her your finger,
She wants your hand.
Once she gets it,
She wants your arm.
Your chest, or even your whole body,
Would not satisfy her;
She wants your soul,
Your brain,
And every inch of your heart.
When she gets
Most of these things,
She feels frustrated;
She feels she has failed,
Because she is no longer
A female protected by a man.
And so she detests the man
Whom she has possessed

And looks for one
Who takes
And who only gives
By studied measure.

With You, I Drown

How shall I describe patience
When it is with you?
How can I express what it is,
When you pay no attention?
How can you tell
That I am persistent and patient?
And if you could tell,
Would you appreciate
That I venture and risk?
How can I explain and illustrate
That with you
On the roads of love, I am
Stupid, dull, and half-witted;
I take half a step
Forward
And ten steps
Backward.

With you I am
Afraid, hesitant, and bashful.
With you
I do not comprehend signs,
Nor understand hints,
And I drown in water
No more than one foot deep.

With you I cannot tell,
I find it impossible to distinguish
Which colour signifies
Progress and advance
And which means
Pausing and waiting.
As for indolent yellow,
The color of readiness and alertness,
It is for me

Like a sea, like ink imprisoned
In a lost bottle
Carried by a current
To an unknown sea.
The only thing left for me with you
Is patience and hope,
And hope with you
Is a ghost with the mask of illusion,
While patience with you
Is the same as a hot meal
Of sand and ashes.

Fed Up With Questions, You Fake the Answers

You have captured my love,
Stolen my reason,
Carried my heart with you,
And now you reveal it to lovers,
Boasting that you have it.
You arrogantly swagger,
Vainly turn around,
And sing a triumphant song
Over my parts,
My torn-off limbs.

I believe you have forgotten –
Oh yes, you have –
That it was my eyes
That highlighted your charm and beauty.
You must have overlooked –
I am sure you have –
That it was my water
That brought your soil to life.
Haven't my flowers grown
In your desert?
Hasn't your breeze smelled
The fragrance of my scent?
Haven't your griefs been intoxicated
With the wine of my love?
Haven't your sorrows
Committed suicide
On the shores of my joy?
Hasn't your passion burned
In the heart of my sun?
Hasn't my full moon risen
In your sky?

And my chest,
Haven't you calmed down,
Relaxed,
Slept for ages
On my chest?

Like them, you recoil
At reproof;
Like them, you close
All doors in my face:
Like the first and the last.
You are a female, and like all females,
You're pleased with words of praise,
You're highly exhilarated
By a touch of the hand,
And you willingly yield
After a sentence of love talk.
You are a belle, and like all belles,
You're tired of questions,
So you fake the answers,
You yield to your imagination
And dreams,
And you feed on lies
In order to live with illusions.

If You Leave Me

If you leave me
In spring
When the air is fragrant
With the perfumes of nature,
Take with you the birds
And the swallows which sing
With happiness and joy,
For I am now sad
And in my heart I feel certain
That they will follow you.
Joy will leave with you,
Pleasure will follow you,
My spring will turn pale,
It will skip the burning heat
And prevent summer
From approaching
Or coming.
And my autumn will arrive
Too early.

Flowers will be too embarrassed
To bloom;
They will fade in all seasons
And under all conditions,
Green grass will go on strike
And refuse to grow
Even in summer.
Tall trees will cry.
As you depart, you will hear
A musical piece,
Familiar to all lovers,
Sighing, gasping,
And then crying
In the valleys of the pain
Which is mixed with separation,

Having the same soil.

You left me and departed,
And autumn whispered in my ear,
Eagerly asking,
'What would you like?
Do you want me to be over?
Don't you want to enjoy
The music of sorrow?
Don't you like colours
When they are dying,
While they cry
Before they fall
And be run over and crushed
By winter?
Tell me frankly, what do you want?
Would you like me
To set the storms,
Cold, and snow of winter
Upon the woman who left you?
Would you like me
To drown her
In my sorrow?
Would you like her to be sleepy?
Would you like her to be asleep?
Would you like her to be nude?
Or would you want her
When winter is over?'

Oh, yes I want her.
I want her to be back
With the coming of spring.
Oh, no, no, I hate it;
She deserted me
While I was enveloped by it,
While it was with me.
No, no, I do not want her
In summer.
And don't ask me
About autumn;
Nor even mention

The word 'winter.'
I want her in
A new season
That does not exist,
My own new season.

My new season,
One that I have invented;
I make it sit or make it stand;
I knead and flatten it;
In it I plant my roses;
In it I grow my vines,
My wheat and barley;
In it I mix my drink
With extraordinary colours
Like those of a rainbow;
I drink it alone,
And alone I dwell in my land;
Alone I enjoy my season.
I make the moon my ship,
The winds my sea,
The sun my oar,
Lightning my smile,
And thunder my guffaw,
While I am alone.
I do not want her with me.
I want her to come
With no companion
In an elegant, decorated casket,
In order to bury her
In my season,
Which I invented
All alone.

I Love You

I could not believe
When I saw you
That you are the same woman
I know.
I have known you
To be cruel,
Unfair,
Unfriendly,
Without tenderness.

You wonder and seem astonished!
Oh, no, no;
The two of us have agreed
On two things:
The first is that I should change,
And the other is that you should accept
My injustice and cruelty,
My madness and revolt,
And a little bit of my ...
Femininity.

But how can you change
So fast?
How can you, a guilty person,
Suddenly become so tender?
And how about your femininity?
When did your masculine qualities
Disappear?
Now I can only see
The female in you!

Willingly and with full conviction,
I have torn off and burned
My false mask
With which I defended myself

Against a society which feared
To submit to the truth
And accept what is right.
In you I have found
A real man
And a true human being,
So I have broken the agreement,
Torn up all the documents
And all the papers
To reveal my true self,
Because I am in love with you.
. . . ?!
I love you.

I Look Down, I Behave Arrogantly

I changed women
The same way I changed clothes
Every day.
I could not stand being intimate
With any female
For more than one day.
Eve was a rib of mine,
And I had the full right
To choose of my ribs
The one I desired
Every day.

My problem was that
I ran out of ribs.
I was intimate with each
Scores of times,
Till my desire began to vomit
At the sight of my ribs
And subsided
Out of boredom.

That was in my youth
When my drink was
Virgin wine
And my food
Wild game,
When I tottered
Like an Arabian horse
Which is devoured by looks,
Yet winks fail to trick it
And not even one hundred looks
Can catch it in a trap

But now
Youth has gone,

And my ribs are
More like sisters and aunts.
I look at all the ribs,
The legitimate and the forbidden,
With sighs and regret,
Realizing how I looked down at,
And behaved arrogantly with,
All ribs,
The legitimate and the forbidden.

This Is My Tragedy

The road with me for you is
A one-way street;
You cannot turn back.
You may contemplate
Slowing down,
But you cannot go back.
It is you who have chosen
This road
With all the clubs and cabarets
It has
And with all the tragedies and disasters
It has.
I have warned you
Not to come along with me,
But you have determined
To stay with me
From the beginning
To the end.

The road with me for you is
A one-way road,
And I am bound
With all roads
And with all teams
To walk
As if I would walk on
To the last step
And to drink,
As if I were a drunkard,
To the last drop.
I cannot choose to go back,
Nor even to stop,
On any road.

The road with me for you is

The same as for every foolish female,
Every beauty who walks with pride,
Belittles the passage of days,
Underestimates dangers,
Ridicules experience,
And finds amusement in watching
Roads and streets,
Indifferent to consequences,
Paying no attention
To the traps set
On all roads
And all streets.

With me you are
Like all females,
As if all of them were with me,
All of them in a wake with me.
But I cannot be
A prisoner
For one female
On all roads;
I cannot hide
In those hideouts
With one female,
Nor walk on, never to go back,
In alleys, lanes,
And streets,
Accompanied by one female.
This is my law;
This is may tragedy:
I am male and you are female,
And a male cannot be satisfied
With one female,
Especially when he walks,
On and on,
On roads, alleys, lanes, and streets,
Which are one-way only.

PART EIGHT

Characters and Images

Tyrants

A tyrant, any tyrant,
Believes,
Whether he was a dwarf
Or a giant,
Whether he is in a bankrupt
Or wealthy country,
Whether his tyranny is exercised
From a camp in the wilderness
Or from a very expensive
Palace –
Tyrants everywhere
And in all times
Believe that they are Gods,
That their retinues
Are angels,
That the Book of Time
Will ever be open
At their pages,
That places would not change
Because they are there.
They believe that although they may
Get sick,
Recovery is fast,
Certain, and guaranteed,
And they will last and last.

They forget or ignore death
And the accounting and torture
That follow death.
Poets and scribes write for them
Odes on constancy and immortality,
Both in verse and prose,
Which are no better than scum.
A tyrant thinks only
Of one thing,

Which physicians work for
When there is a single male
And a countless number
Of females.
They prescribe for him
All kinds of concoctions
And tonics.

If a tyrant seeks advice,
The evil entourage of counselors
Give him back
His own opinions.
If he suspects an individual,
They question the whole nation.
If he decides to throw a person in jail,
They cover the ground with thorns
And surround the whole country with walls.
If he has a yearning for the sight of blood,
They make for him a river
Which flows
With the blood of the innocent.
And if once upon a time
He remembers
To go out among people
Pretending
To worship the Lord of Creation,
This – God save us – means
To hypocrites
Who have sold their faith
That he is doing a favour
To the Lord of Creation
By praying.

When the time arrives
And God answers the prayer
Of a kneeling, oppressed woman
Who has been raped and had her life destroyed,
Of an innocent child
Whose father has been murdered,
Of a young man, full of life,
Who has been tortured

And got lost,
Or of a feeble old man
Who has been deprived of medicine
And of the means to make a living –
When God answers such a prayer,
The tyrant falls down,
A deformed, rotten corpse,
Food for worms;
And he will be tortured
In hell by day and night,
Leaving nothing behind
Other than terrible nightmares
Visited upon those
Who have witnessed and experienced
The rule of the tyrant.

A Tyrant and a Mufti

A tyrant,
Any tyrant with no exception,
Believes
He will never be defeated,
He will not be defeated
By his oppression,
By his hatred,
Or by his guile.
He believes he is full of power and might.

In every age,
Since ancient times,
Tyrants have been a species of men
Who believe only in themselves,
Worship only themselves.
And lose only themselves.
A tyrant believes himself to be
The centre of the universe
And all things and animals
Revolve around him.
He believes in no God.

A tyrant does not know
What kindness means
Nor how tenderness is spelled.
He has never, ever heard
The word tolerance,
Or a sentence that says,
'A compromise must be reached,'
Or the phrase,
'It is better to shake hands.'
He smiles only at sorrow
And laughs only at seeing
Blood and torn limbs.
His retinue are a group of

Human and jinn devils.
His brains are possessed
By the great Satan.
His heart is made of tin
And pumps into his body
Blood made of fire.
He is only inclined
To what is harmful and evil.

A tyrant is like a mufti;
Both take the place of God
As a legislator,
Forbidding things and allowing others.
The first ordains
Decrees against God's Law,
While the other works hard,
Attempting by all means
Not to slip and commit
What God has forbidden.

God will take care
Of both persons.
We cannot tell what God
Will do with the tyrant.
As for an honest mufti,
If he rules correctly,
He has a double reward,
And he has just one
If he errs.
God knows what His creatures are doing.
He does unto them what He likes;
He is capable
Of everything
And has knowledge
Of everything.

Banquet of the Mean

In every frightened country,
Among all terrified nations,
There is one common denominator,
A single rule,
A conspicuous sign,
Which all rulers share
Who grab authority
And take hold of the reins
By force.
The denominator is
Disbelief in God,
The rule is wiping out
Religion and religious belief,
And the sign is
Seizing the wealth and properties
Of people
And closing the borders,
From extreme east to extreme west
And from extreme north to extreme south.
Those living behind
The walls of oppression and injustice
Will have only one job available:
To work as agents and spies,
To be guests at a banquet
Where the hosts are mean
And the food is forbidden.

I Don't Know Why

I don't know why
They say
I am silly,
Gross, and crude,
Although sometimes
I act the role
Of a funny clown,
Or a smiling, kind,
Congenial person.
Most often I
Invent heroic feats
For myself
Which most confidently
I narrate.
If, for instance, the subject of conversation
Is drugs and addiction,
Then I am the man,
The one who has exposed
The most powerful gang
Of drug trafficking.
I also have tried
All kinds of drugs.
I am an expert and an authority
Not, as they say, a stupid beast.
So why do they add to my name
'The low,'
And why do they say
I am crude,
Silly, and gross?
I don't know why!

They call me
The tall-tale man
Of evening gatherings,
Just because I once said,

At an evening party,
When there was a lot of talk
About the invasion of space,
That I am a space expert.
But when the conversation turned
To amorous affairs,
I said that a certain singer
Stopped singing for my sake
And that a particular actress
Was divorced on my account.
I said that because I have
An extensive knowledge
Of science and technology
A deep understanding
Of arts and letters,
And a rich background
In war and politics,
I was offered to be
A close advisor and a cabinet member,
For I have knowledge
In all fields
And am enthusiastic
About every thing.
So why do they add
To my name,
'The tall-tale man,'
Although actually I am
A bold inventor.
Why? Why?
I don't know why.

The Labour of Sedition

These people you find
All over, in streets,
In clubs,
In mosques,
And in our own houses
Among our sons,
Daughters, and grandchildren –
Most of these
Utter harsh, offensive words,
Sharp, poisoned phrases,
Which throw mud
Into the river of our daily life
And assassinate our time.
They are preparing things,
In a most casual manner
As if they knew exactly what they were doing,
Or they are not aware
That they are arranging
For the labour of sedition
And for a great fire.
Most of them are
Boys with no experience.

The most terrible thing,
The greatest catastrophe,
Is that they behave
As if they were gods,
Casting people
To the bottom of Hell,
While this decision
Is for no man to make;
It is the creator's decision.
They charge chaste women
With adultery and lewdness
Without thinking

Or pondering what they are doing.
They prevent wives
From intimacy with their husbands
On the pretext that they are sinners.
They classify people
According to their beard hair:
Woe to a clean-shaved man
Both in his old age
And in his youth,
While one with a loose beard,
Which is never trimmed or combed,
Is one of the pious
And sensible.

God, the Compassionate
And Merciful God,
The Forgiving and Kind,
The only Owner of the universe,
Addresses a message to His servants:
'Say: "Servants of God
Who have sinned against your souls,
Despair not of God's mercy;
He forgives
All sins.
He is the Forgiving One, the Merciful." '
And God
Addresses His prophet,
The master of all creatures
And of all messenger,
God's mercy to all people,
The best promoter of good
And the leading censurer
Of evil
With wisdom and kindly urging,
With most courteous reasoning –
God addresses and orders him:
' "... He who is well guided
Is so for his own benefit,
And he who goes astray
Does so to his own disadvantage."
You are not their keeper.'

And you are not our keepers
Even if most extremely
We go astray.

The Secret

I and the plume
Which is used to play the *'oud*[1]
Share a secret which goes back
To the age of innocence,
The days of childhood,
When my uncle
Used to chant his songs,
Setting afire once more
Hearts that have cooled down,
Filing them again with love
By means of unsurpassed tunes
Which he created with his plume
Inflaming the strings
And setting the *'oud* ablaze
With the sweetest numbers.

My uncle embraced the *'oud*
As if it were his beloved.
His wife was jealous;
She was afraid of the fire
That set the strings aflame,
Afraid it would burn her
And the house.
So my aunt asked me a favour;
She wanted me to find out
What was going on
Between my uncle
And the *'oud* and its strings.

The plume was a child like me.
I innocently asked her,
Imploringly begged her,
To tell me what went on

[1] A musical instrument widely used in the Arab world.

Between my uncle and the *'oud*.
Without hesitation,
Without any hesitation,
She said, 'He orders me,
And I flirt with the strings of love.
He begs me
To strike the strings of passion.
He implores me
To go on,
Not to grow restless
And interrupt
The strings of melancholy.
He beseeches me
To scoop out
Of my spring
Extraordinary, impossible tunes,
Which no lovers on the banks of the Tigris
Have ever thought of,
No composers in the nightclubs of Aleppo
Have ever discovered,
No beauties of Sanaa
Have ever danced to;
Tunes which singers on the banks of the Nile
And patrons of the clubs of Hejaz
Are unaware of;
Tunes that are still in the womb,
Unborn yet,
That were defeated with the surrender,
Got sick after the loss,
Turned old in the diaspora,
And died in the womb of Andalusia.'

I hurried to my aunt
And told her of the conversation
I had with the plume
Which played the *'oud*
Absently she muttered,
'Your uncle must be
Embracing the *'oud*,
While thinking of someone else
Other than me,

A maiden that has been absent
For hundreds of years,
Always repeating her name
In his songs, in his dreams.
A grandfather of his
Was infatuated with this maiden
When he emigrated
Hundreds of years ago
From the closed Hejaz
To the open and remote Morocco.
He followed the beautiful maiden
And disappeared, in the unknown,
In Andalusia.
No news were heard of him ever since,
And no one has discovered
Since then
Her obstinate secret
Or his remote one.'

Index of First Lines

A starving *dog* followed me, 58
At the peak of my anger, 124
A tyrant, 182
A tyrant, any tyrant, 179

Day after day, I read xiii
Do you know 80
During my calm, 110

Eve, full of hope and joy, 143
Every day, without failing, 36

Folks, people, 51
Freedom? 75

He asked her, 73
How seconds make 131
How shall I describe patience 163

I adore the brush 128
I am a father of six girls. 141
I am cold and inert 88
I am going to die 107
I and the plume. 190
I catch my breath and think 85
I changed women 172
I could not believe 170
I did not consult my brain 90
I don't know why 185
If you leave me 167
I hate my memory. 7
I look for the unknown, 65
In every frightened country, 184
In every terrified country, 60
In my contradictory evenings, 121
In my imagination and in reality, 103
I now loathe ornaments; 158
Insolent and shameless was I, 4
I remembered and missed you 156
'I see under the ashes, 56
I work hard and toil. 105

Let us begin 17
Let us imagine life 69
Loneliness used to torment me. 100
Love asked me, 149
Love on my pillow, 153

My belief in life and existence 3
My beloved, xi
My joys and my smiles 115
My poems make you jealous; 151
My ship went too far 108

No to words! 71

O my eternal yearning 92
Once I decided 83
Our Author and Creator 82

Suddenly, while I was at the climax 109

The road with me for you is 174
The same way that it happens 78
These people you find 187
The way you received ix
They said about love 67
They say 119
Tyrants are only made 54

When I am fully awake 6
When I am with you I feel 137
When I sleep I am attacked 112
When I was a teenager 160
When my tears had dried, 97
Who was it that made my grief? 113

You approach! 144
You get lost in the valley of anxiety, 145
You have captured my love, 165

You have contrived a plot 147   You provoke my jealousy, 125
You lie when you say 139   Your anniversary, beloved, 38
You my heart, submerged 11   Your eyes are a wide and 154